Sustainable Coffee in Costa Rica

Sustainable Coffee in Costa Rica

Solutions for People, Economic Development, and Biodiversity

Andrew P. Miller and Jeffrey A. Stratford

BLOOMSBURY ACADEMIC
NEW YORK • LONDON • OXFORD • NEW DELHI • SYDNEY

BLOOMSBURY ACADEMIC
Bloomsbury Publishing Inc, 1359 Broadway, New York, NY 10018, USA
Bloomsbury Publishing Plc, 50 Bedford Square, London, WC1B 3DP, UK
Bloomsbury Publishing Ireland, 29 Earlsfort Terrace, Dublin 2, D02 AY28, Ireland

BLOOMSBURY, BLOOMSBURY ACADEMIC and the Diana logo are trademarks of Bloomsbury Publishing Plc

First published in the United States of America 2025

Library of Congress Cataloging-in-Publication Data available

ISBN: HB: 978-1-6669-1279-1
ePDF: 979-8-7651-5505-9
eBook: 978-1-6669-1280-7

Typeset by Deanta Global Publishing Services, Chennai, India

For product safety related questions contact productsafety@bloomsbury.com.

To find out more about our authors and books visit www.bloomsbury.com and sign up for our newsletters.

The world loves coffee. We love coffee. But we also love the people of Costa Rica as well the incredible diversity found in the Costa Rican landscape. The goal of our book is to show not only the importance of coffee, but how conservation and coffee can go hand in hand with increasing living standards. This book is a celebration of a combined fifty years of working in Costa Rica and other tropical countries. We appreciate the hospitality repeatedly demonstrated by our Costa Rican friends and the patience of our wives. We dedicate this work to the students of Wilkes University, especially those that trusted us with their first trip out of the country or even their first time in a plane. We wish you great success and a passport filled with stamped pages. We raise our mugs to you.

Contents

Introduction

The Importance of the Coffee Industry to International Political Economy

This book examines the coffee industry in Costa Rica and the complex ways in which politics, society, economic development, and ecological issues intersect. As most college students cramming for an exam know, coffee is a very important part of many people's lives. In fact, the National Coffee Association reports that 62 percent of Americans drink coffee each day, even exceeding the consumption of tap water (prnewswire.com)! Despite the centrality of coffee consumption to many people's lives, few understand where it comes from, how it is produced, and the amount of work it takes to create their morning cup of coffee. This book seeks to provide an understanding of the complexities of the coffee industry and the myriad ways in which we are connected to it in our daily lives. Furthermore, this book will also examine the interplay between the long-term economic sustainability of the coffee industry in Costa Rica and long-term ecological sustainability, the ecological impacts of the coffee industry, and the historic role of coffee in Costa Rican politics, culture, and society. The issues of economic and ecological sustainability in coffee production are important to the long-term social and political stability of the coffee industry and the people who have dedicated their lives to it. In order for coffee to have a sustainable future, there needs to be strategies that integrate policies that promote the long-term profitability of coffee farming, including ecological management techniques to continue to have the sort of yields that provide for a steady income.

Throughout the history of Latin America, coffee has served as a central but often unstable economic enterprise that many rely on for their livelihoods, most especially in rural areas that are often economically underdeveloped. The question at the heart of this book is what factors contribute to the long-term economic success as well as political and social stability of the coffee industry in Costa Rica. The central argument of this book is that long-term economic success for the Costa Rican coffee industry is enhanced and catalyzed by economic, social, political, and especially ecological sustainability. We define ecological sustainability as the use of a renewable resource without continuous declines in that resource or increasing negative impacts on biodiversity and ecosystem services.

Since coffee is one of the most traded commodities on the international market, its impact on the everyday lives of the people who produce it is enormous. The problems faced by coffee farmers are further exacerbated by the fact that the vast majority of the world's coffee is grown in developing countries where the coffee trade makes up a large amount of the total trade and there are few other economic opportunities. In addition, unlike many other agricultural products, coffee tends to be grown on small farm plots with around 25 million farming households accounting for about 80 percent of the total output (FAO 2023). It is also important to note that while the vast majority of coffee is produced in the developing world, the majority of it is consumed in the developed world. As such, it is important to understand the economic impact of the coffee trade on the places that produce it and the best strategies to increase the long-term viability of the coffee industry. Social stability for the coffee industry is reinforced by measures that improve market stability via ecological management policies that make year-to-year harvests more predictable so farm families can have a more stable source of income. Political stability will be improved by government policies that empower coffee farmers rather than seeing them as a source of tax revenue or as atavism that should recede to the background of Costa Rican economic policy.

Due to the fact that most of the world's coffee production is skewed toward much smaller operations than many other agricultural operations, this further intensifies the importance in many of the world's poorest countries. Approximately 125 million people worldwide depend on coffee to make a living, with small and often family-run farms producing about 80 percent of coffee production spread across 25 million smallholders (Fair Trade UK). Consequently, the impact of a difficult coffee-growing season or a decline in the price of coffee tends to be more acute among groups that are the least likely to withstand it. The importance of coffee to Latin America cannot be overstated, as the tradition of coffee production in the region runs deep and many countries have long depended on coffee production as a major export crop.

> Coffee is a particularly important commodity for analysis not only because it has been one of the world's most valuable internationally traded goods for the past two centuries, but because Latin America has dominated production. At one time or another, in the nineteenth and twentieth centuries, coffee was the leading export of nearly half the countries of the Americas and an important secondary crop in a number of others. (Topik and Samper 2006, 119)

For much of its history, coffee was an outsized part of the Costa Rican economy and society. Though its importance has diminished somewhat over time, coffee continues to be an important export and the sole livelihood of many people who live in coffee-growing regions. For instance, in Costa Rica during the 2019–2020 growing season, there were 38,804 coffee farmers utilizing 93,697 hectares of land to produce 1,472,366 60-KG bags of coffee that were exported to the following countries: the United States (47.7 percent), followed by Belgium (17.5 percent), Germany (6.6 percent), and South Korea (4 percent) (Gonzalez 2020). At the aggregate level, the scale of Costa Rican coffee production has dipped since the mid-twentieth century due to various factors; however, it is important to understand that coffee farming is highly localized and concentrated in a handful of areas in the country, which means that in places like the Los Santos region, which include the famous Tarrazú and Dota coffee-growing regions, coffee production is easily the most important economic activity and is linked to the livelihoods of nearly the entire population. Due to this, it is important to analyze the various risks to coffee production from pests and diseases as well as the volatility of the market.

THE ECONOMIC IMPORTANCE OF THE COFFEE INDUSTRY

One of the most important problems facing coffee farmers is the volatility of the market due to the usual issues inherent in agricultural production, such as weather conditions, pests, and diseases. Despite the benefits for coffee farmers in being connected to the global trading system, one of the main sources of economic angst among coffee farmers is the problem of market volatility. While market volatility is an issue with agro-exports generally, coffee production is often more acutely affected by it due to the nature of coffee growing. First, since the coffee harvest is spread over 3–4 months, there is a lot of time for weather and pests to decrease the yield. Secondly, the emergence of new competitors growing large amounts of coffee has affected the supply chain, often causing a glut of coffee.

Given the amount of coffee produced on small, family-run farms, extreme price volatility is especially detrimental to the coffee industry because price instability often makes it difficult to interpret the price signals necessary to efficiently manage their operations. Since coffee is a crop grown in many parts of the world, it is essentially impossible for coffee producers to react to short-term fluctuations in price and adapt accordingly. This is further aggravated by the fact that coffee is grown by small producers who are not as connected to the international market and therefore not in a position to make rapid policy changes based on market changes. This means that volatility in the market has a number of negative effects, including the inability to predict future income, which will often manifest itself in difficulties in long-range planning. Williamson (2012) argues that there is "abundant contemporary microeconomic evidence linking income volatility to lower investment in physical capital, human capital, and even research and development. In addition, the less-risky investment that does take place in the presence of price volatility tends to be low return. Lower investment and lower returns on less investment" (197). Lower investment in a coffee operation will often lead to lower yields year over year as the coffee bushes generally take about five years to produce at peak efficiency and then slow down after about three decades of production. To combat this phenomenon, coffee farmers often put seedlings into a nursery to replace older coffee bushes at the end of their productive lifespan, so that the coffee farm has as many highly productive plants as possible. Here again, there is a more pronounced effect in poorer countries as they are more risk-averse to replacing large portions of a coffee plantation and potentially seeing a short-term downturn in production. In more developed coffee-producing countries like Costa Rica, many coffee farmers have the capital to replace coffee bushes on a rotating basis and are less risk-averse in doing so. In addition, this process is labor-intensive and expensive, but this type of investment ensures the farm is as productive as possible. When market volatility discourages investment, it creates a vicious cycle of lack of investment, lower yields, and lower profitability for the farmer, which leads back to lack of investment.

Despite some farmers in Costa Rica replacing their coffee bushes on a rotating basis, this phenomenon can clearly be seen in Costa Rica as crop yields have diminished over time. For instance, the USDA (2022) reports that coffee yields decreased by 7 percent for MY 2021–2022 because "aging plantations yielded less volume and higher incidence of fungal diseases affected coffee cherry development in early stages in key growing areas." In addition, volatility in the coffee market often comes from the unpredictability of weather conditions and the constant pressure of pests and disease on coffee production, with older plants more susceptible to disease. Prime among them is the fungus known as "coffee rust," or *roya* in Latin America. In the last twenty years, there have been at least two outbreaks of the fungus that have devastated coffee-growing areas of Central America.

> Roya first broke out in the region in 2012, and by 2014, over half of the coffee crops had been affected, before it was largely brought under control. The humidity brought by the two hurricanes of 2020, which themselves wreaked $3.3 billion worth of damage to regional economies, boosted the prevalence of the disease from low single digit percentages of coffee plants in the 2019/20 season to 15-25% in 2020/21, according to industry data. (Reuters 2021)

Diseases such as *roya* also tend to be more devastating in poorer countries and among farmers least able to fight it. In more economically developed coffee-growing countries such as Costa Rica, coffee farmers often (but not always) have access to more tools to fight diseases and pests as well as access to better technical assistance. For instance, during the 2012–2014 outbreak, around half of El Salvador's coffee plants were affected by *roya*, in Guatemala it was approximately 40 percent, and in Honduras about 10 percent of coffee plants were affected. This outbreak in *roya* also corresponded with a nearly 50 percent decrease in coffee prices in U.S. markets (Reuters 2013). Obviously, considerably lower production coupled with much lower prices had a major negative impact on those who rely on coffee farming for their livelihoods.

Problems of volatility and lack of investment are further exacerbated by the difficulty many coffee farmers face in taking advantage of value-added services that would increase their incomes. Not only has the difficulty of creating value-added benefits for those who produce the coffee hampered their ability to make a larger profit, it has also greatly skewed the income distribution of coffee farmers to the places where coffee is consumed, as about 70 percent of the income from the coffee trade goes to the developed world, with other 30 percent staying in the developing world. Even of the 30 percent that stays in the developing world, only between 7 percent and 10 percent of total income goes to the actual farm family (Mata and Hernández-Ruiz 2019, 88). Again, phenomena such as this are also more acutely felt by farmers in the poorest coffee-producing countries, who have the most difficulty in creating value-added services that increase their bottom line.

That is not to say that farmers have not found interesting ways to increase value-added services and, therefore, their own percentage of profit. There are some producers that have found unusual niche markets for their products to boost their own percentage of the profits. The niche markets are often based either on a geographical designation or some sort of unique processing technique. Some of the most well-known high-end varietals carry a geographic designation, such as Jamaican Blue Mountain and Hawaiian Kona, which require a very explicit set of processing procedures and are only grown in a very specific part of a country's coffee region. Due to the cost of these coffees (often ranging from $80 to $100 per pound), there are many knockoffs and counterfeits, which encouraged Jamaica and Hawaii to tightly regulate exactly what constitutes the Blue Mountain and Kona brands. For Jamaican Blue Mountain, the coffee must be grown in the Blue Mountains, and Kona must be produced solely in the Kona region of Hawaii.

Another way that some producers have tried to favorably position their coffee in the international market is by having some sort of (sometimes unusual) niche. The most prominent examples of this are kopi luwak (sometimes referred to as civet coffee), produced first in Indonesia but now spreading to other locations in Southeast Asia, and Monsooned Malabar, produced in India. Kopi luwak is particularly interesting as it is gathered from the excrement of a small weasellike animal called a civet, then washed, processed, and roasted into one of the world's most expensive coffees. Not for the faint of heart, when the civet plucks a (supposedly) perfectly ripe coffee bean and ingests it, "their digestive enzymes change the structure of proteins in the coffee beans, which removes some of the acidity to make a smoother cup of coffee" (Bale 2016).

Civets have long been considered a pest in Indonesian coffee fields, so initially the discovery that coffee could be salvaged from their droppings and sold as an extremely expensive product helped mediate the conflict between the animals and human farmers. As the coffee has become more popular as a strange novelty, many people have become concerned about the treatment of the civets, who no longer roam the fields in search of ripe coffee cherries but instead are confined to tiny cages and fed a diet solely consisting of coffee cherries to produce as much kopi luwak as possible (Bale 2016).

While kopi luwak depends on the digestive systems of civets, Monsoon Malabar depends on the monsoon rains that fall on India each year. After the coffee is picked, it is processed more or less as any coffee would be. However, the unique part of Monsoon Malabar is that it is exposed to the yearly monsoon rains, which cause the beans to swell and alter their flavor profile when roasted and brewed. Monsoon Malabar is produced in the following manner:

> The natural monsooning process is streamlined with strict quality control to make Monsoon Malabar coffee. The process begins with the grading of the green coffee beans which are then exposed to the warm and humid Indian monsoon winds during the monsoon months of June to September in aerated warehouses on the Malabar coast. The coffee is regularly turned as it absorbs moisture from the air. This results in a unique smooth brew with the least acidity and slightly weathered taste which you can't find in any other coffee in the world. (Naivo Café)

Costa Rican coffee producers have used some innovative production practices to boost sales and to create a value-added product. However, Costa Rican farmers have mainly focused on the production of coffee that will receive a premium price due to quality, which is a relatively recent phenomenon.

> There have been relevant changes in the role of coffee producers (in Costa Rica), going from a producer–harvester to a producer who can also process with a focus on quality. This change places Costa Rica as one of the world's most excellent coffee producers. Differentiated, high-quality coffee recognizes the site-specific production, processing, and commercialization of coffee with a premium price liquidation. In addition, high quality coffee depends on specific geographic conditions, which must be understood to characterize the geographic and productive changes in the coffee sector. (Quesada-Román, Quirós-Arias and Zamora-Pereira 2022, 2)

The focus on quality has also meant that the majority of Costa Rican coffee generally and almost all of the high-quality coffee are slated for export, with the majority of exports to the United States and the rest to other developed countries (table I.1).

It is common throughout the agricultural supply chain for Costa Rica to export its top-quality products abroad while keeping the imperfect items for domestic consumption. For things like mangoes, pineapples, or papaya the fruit often has some sort of cosmetic defect but is otherwise perfectly edible. Coffee, on the other hand, could have some cosmetic issues; however, low-quality coffee usually comes from defects caused by insects or disease but is most often caused by too many unripe coffee cherries in the process. This can be due to poor picking or coffee picked at the end of the season when all coffee cherries are harvested regardless of ripeness. This sort of coffee makes up the vast majority of the harvest that is used for domestic consumption. Interestingly, the percentage of coffee that is export quality does not leave enough low-quality coffee for domestic consumption, which actually necessitates the importation of coffee from its neighbors. Given the amount of coffee produced in Costa Rica, it is remarkable to note that:

Table I.1 Exports of Green Coffee (60-KG Bags)

Destination	*Yr. 2019/2020*	*Yr. 2020/2021*	*Yr. 2021/2022*
United States	559,427	490,813	506,264
Belgium	224.033	286,583	227,794
Germany	63,180	79,658	62,168
South Korea	44,413	31,959	43,483
Spain	27,279	29,258	15,497
Israel	25.026	25,026	17,659
Italy	32,481	23,509	22,042
Others	168,484	183,350	161,514
Total	1,139,206	1,150,156	1,056,431

Source: Costa Rican Coffee Institute (ICAFE) and Costa Rican Customs Department, via USDA (2023).

> Costa Rica started to import economically significant volumes of coffee in 2008, primarily from other Central American countries (e.g., Honduras and Nicaragua), to meet part of its domestic consumption needs. Since most of Costa Rica's coffee is priced at a premium in the international markets, most locally produced coffee is exported, with lower priced Costa Rican coffee remaining in the local market. Since 2008, imports have fluctuated widely, responding to local roasters' ability to maximize profits through imports based on pricing, availability, and logistics. Imports of roasted coffee have increased over time, representing 14 percent of total imports during MY 2021/22. (USDA 2023)

Not surprisingly, the concept of quality in the coffee industry is fraught with issues of interpretation and subjectivity, despite attempts to make the process as objective as possible by setting industry-wide testing standards. These standards judge coffee on two main parameters, each with sub-parameters that delve deeper into the coffee variety and the manner in which it was produced. The material quality of coffee is therefore determined by the inherent quality of the coffee bean, species, variety, soil, environmental conditions, etc., as well as external quality factors such as how it is farmed, harvested, and processed.

The most prestigious coffee competition in the world is known as the Cup of Excellence (CoE), which was created in 1999 to assess the quality of coffee in the emerging high-end coffee market. Since the majority of high-quality coffee is grown by small producers, the CoE has a particularly strong impact on smaller operations.

> Smallholder farmers gain the most from Cup of Excellence since historically they had the least education in recognizing their own quality and much less power in demanding fair value. Most coffees were blended- higher qualities were mixed with other lower quality coffees in order to push to a medium quality. While there was often no malicious intent since blending was the standard it benefitted the larger commercial exporters and importers. (Cup of Excellence 2023)

Inspired by the traditions surrounding wine tasting, Cup of Excellence assesses coffee quality across the following parameters: fragrance/aroma, acidity (intensity), body (heavy to thin), uniformity, clean cup (no non-coffee or off-flavors), sweetness, and then subtractions for defects (CoE 2023). To be included in the CoE, farmers submit their own samples to CoE for judging. It is important to point out that as the specialty coffee market has expanded in the last few years, it is quite common for coffee producers, even very smallholders, to submit their coffee to competitions and also to send it to boutique coffee roasters in the United States and Europe unsolicited to ask them to try the sample in hopes of selling directly to the roaster. Once the CoE has coffee samples, all of them are tasted and the group is pared down to 150 coffees. From there, they are further judged round by round with the highest scoring coffee advancing from the original group to 150, ninety, forty, and finally to thirty different coffees. There is then an awards ceremony for the ranked top 30, and finally, the coffee is sold at auction with prices typically far above the New York Stock Exchange price. It is estimated that this process takes the equivalent of 8,720 cups of coffee to complete (CoE 2023).

While the development of more highly differentiated and high-quality coffee varieties has improved the profit margins for many Costa Rican farmers, even the extra amount paid to many of them based on higher levels of quality does not always solve what has come to be known as the coffee paradox. "The coffee paradox is the phenomenon by which the coffee prices received by farmers/producers in developing countries have been increasingly lower, despite a growing demand for this product" (Mata and Hernández-Ruiz 2019, 85). One of the main drivers of the coffee paradox is the pricing and growing popularity of coffee-based drinks that use small amounts of coffee and charge a high price relative to the amount of coffee consumed. For instance, a Starbucks frappuccino contains an amount of caffeine equal to about 1.5 tablespoons of coffee, while a 20-ounce Starbucks brewed coffee requires about five tablespoons of coffee but costs about half as much. Put another way, the value added by chains such as Starbucks is able to take a raw material purchased at between $1.00 and $2.50 a pound depending on current prices on the stock exchange and convert 1.5 tablespoons into a $5 drink. There is also a tendency for small luxury items like fancy coffee drinks to have an inelastic demand curve, meaning that increases in price do not have a strong effect on consumer demand and can often boost a company's profit margin. Research also shows that Starbucks price increases can actually lead to more consumption as it increases the perception of Starbucks coffee as a premium brand. "Rather than trying to compete with cheaper chains like Dunkin', Starbucks uses price hikes to separate itself from the pack and reinforce the premium image of their brand and products. Since their loyal following isn't especially price sensitive, Starbucks coffee maintains a fairly inelastic demand curve, and a small price increase can have a huge positive impact on their margins without decreasing demand for beverages" (Paddle 2020). In this way, coffee shops outside of coffee-growing regions are able to capture an outsized percentage of the coffee market via value-added services.

THE PURSUIT OF A VALUE-ADDED COFFEE PRODUCT

Costa Rica has the advantage of a growing environment that creates very high-quality coffee, and they have used this ability to grow very high-quality beans to create their own niche and differentiation in the coffee market. Product differentiation based on quality is not a new concept, and one of the first coffee-producing countries in Latin America to actively market their coffee as higher quality was Colombia, who developed a highly successful strategy of product differentiation focused on the quality of Colombian coffee, which subsequently led to brand recognition as high-quality (Forero 2010, 103). Costa Rica, similarly to Colombia, does not have a gimmicky niche, so the focus on quality centers on the cultivation of desirable high-quality varietals and processing methods that help to create unique flavors. A study by Traore, Wilson, and Fields (2018) "revealed cuppers', buyers', and therefore consumers' preferences for coffee material attributes such as aromas and flavors. Results show that fruity, floral, sweet, spice, and sour acid aromas and flavors are the favorite flavors and aromas. Also, the analysis reveals that buyers (consumers) prefer balanced coffee. The recognition of these material attributes is important especially for coffee buyers because it allows them to buy high-quality coffees" (366).

Over the last couple of decades, Costa Rica has positioned itself as a purveyor of high-quality coffee by trying to market Tarrazú coffee as a region that routinely produces great coffee and through the use of luxury coffee varieties that can command a higher price, such as the increasingly popular Gesha variety. Gesha has spread rapidly in Costa Rica and Panama and has an increasingly impressive track record in national and international coffee competitions, including winning nineteen of the top thirty spots at the International Cup of Excellence competition for Costa Rica (cupofexcellence .org). Even more striking is that just two years prior to that, at a coffee auction in 2019, Panamanian Gesha sold for $1029 a pound (de León 2020), so it appears that the sky's the limit for the most highly sought-after luxury coffees. In fact, the specialty coffee market has increased its market share from about 1 percent to over 25 percent since the late 1990s (Traore, Wilson, and Fields 2018, 350). The luxury coffee market is further facilitated by the manner in which coffee is processed, which can influence the taste of the final product. One of the most popular processing methods for luxury coffee is the process that creates what is known as honey coffee. When coffee fruit is dried in the sun, some of the sweetness of the fruit adheres to the expelled coffee seed and creates a cup of coffee that is smoother, sweeter, more desirable, and consequently, more expensive. The popularity of these luxury coffees has exploded over the last decade or so, particularly in the Asian market, and many experts believe that the sector will continue to grow. Since honey coffee is a process rather than a coffee varietal, it has the added benefit of working with many different types of coffee during processing and is an excellent value-added option for coffee farmers and processors.

The majority of coffee is exported unroasted because coffee quality declines rapidly after roasting, and even faster after grinding; therefore, coffee is typically roasted closer to the source of retail. In addition, large coffee companies such as Starbucks and Seattle's Best want to be able to roast the coffee themselves for consistency of flavor in the final product. Smaller boutique coffee companies that are roasting coffee for the luxury market are especially interested in roasting it themselves to ensure that the coffee is properly roasted for its flavor profile. In general, this means that coffee from Costa Rica is normally produced as a light roast to enhance the acidity and citric quality of the coffee.

Despite the fact that many of the large contracts with coffee cooperatives and *beneficios* require them to export their coffee unroasted, there is a lot of money to be made in the added value of roasting it themselves. For instance, for a $2.80 cup of coffee, $0.07 goes to the farmer, $0.16 to the exporter, $0.35 to the roaster, $0.04 to the distributor, and $2.17 to the retailer (World Economic Forum 2020). Not only does roasting the final product increase the amount of profit significantly, but bringing as many of the phases of the coffee process into a single enterprise will also boost profits. The problem, however, is that by far the largest amount of money for a cup of coffee goes to the retail outlet. The problem for coffee facilities in Costa Rica and elsewhere is that a retail outlet in-country will serve a limited number of customers since it is naturally only accessible to the people who live near it. That said, many coffee operations in Costa Rica have a retail outlet that does a bustling local business and will often further supplement those sales with online sales in order to send their coffee around the world.

FAIR TRADE CERTIFICATION

Some individual coffee farmers, as well as some coffee cooperatives in Costa Rica, will also pursue a Fair Trade certification as a way to create added value. Under these programs, extra money is conferred through a Fair Trade premium provided by the certifying organization directly to the farmer. In addition, these programs also try to create a more stable price structure due to the creation of a minimum price for coffee regardless of the prevailing market price. One of the most well-known Fair Trade organizations is Fair Trade International, which has a multipronged approach to Fair Trade certification, including the following:

1. Prices that aim to cover the average costs of producing their crop sustainably—a vital safety net when market prices drop.
2. The Fairtrade Premium—an extra sum of money paid on top of the selling price to invest in business or community projects of their choice.
3. Decent working conditions and a ban on discrimination, forced labor, and child labor.
4. Access to advance credit ahead of harvest time.
5. Being able to plan more for the future with more security and stronger relationships with buyers (Fair Trade UK, https://www.fairtrade.org.uk/farmers-and-workers/coffee).

While the goals of Fair Trade are certainly admirable and provide some level of benefit to many coffee farmers, the positive effects of certification are limited. The coffee growers who do sell to Fair Trade cooperatives often do so in order to offload lower quality coffee that is not up to the standards of prominent roasters in the export market. This is because the quality of the coffee sold to the Fair Trade organization often does not meet market standards for quality and therefore has to be sold on an alternative market such as Fair Trade since quality is not a factor in the transaction and the Fair Trade premium is a welcome addition to the price. Dragusanu, Montero, and Nunn (2021), in interviews with Costa Rican coffee farmers, found that many of them sell to Fair Trade organizations "as a strategy that is often pursued by producers who would have difficulty selling their coffee otherwise" (2). Due to this, Fair Trade coffee also tends to be of lower quality, which hurts the specialty market further by providing lower quality coffee at an inflated price.

Even when farmers sell their coffee via Fair Trade, most Fair Trade premiums paid to farmers are often largely inconsequential and provide only a small benefit. For instance, Vogt (2019) found that the Fair Trade premium was, in most cases, allocated to supplemental incomes. Where used for community development projects, developing community infrastructure was often favored, such as a football field. (170) We found a similar use of the Fair Trade premium during our work in the Los Santos region of Costa Rica when the entire year's Fair Trade premium was used to buy new trash cans for the local high school.

SUSTAINABLE AND ORGANIC COFFEE CERTIFICATIONS

In addition to Fair Trade certifications, there are also a number of certification schemes for sustainability to demonstrate sustainable practices, including Rainforest Alliance, 4C, and UTZ, which can add value for producers.

Additionally, some large corporations such as Nestle and Starbucks have their own in-house sustainability certification criteria. These sorts of schemes are often popular with consumers as the area of coffee managed under voluntary sustainability standards (Harvey et al. 2021) has increased (Willer, Lernoud, and Kemper 2018). However, the effectiveness of certification on biodiversity is highly variable (Harvey et al. 2021).

The Rainforest Alliance, which is one of the most popular sustainability certifications, examines coffee producers via four main criteria: forests, climate, human rights, and livelihood. They provide training in addition to certification regarding best practices for forest management that include forest protection, strategies to prevent the expansion of farmland into additional forest areas, and strategies to manage the soil and other agricultural inputs. The climate component helps to avoid deforestation and to increase land management techniques that increase carbon storage and decrease greenhouse gas emissions. In addition to the ecological training and certification goals, the Rainforest Alliance also incorporates human rights, in the context of coffee farming, rights of people in rural areas, and provides robust strategies assessing and addressing child labor, forced labor, poor working conditions, low wages, gender inequality, and the violation of Indigenous land rights. Their approach also seeks to lift people out of poverty via the financial benefits that come with certification (Rainforest Alliance).

Many Costa Rican coffee farmers will also seek to have their coffee production certified as being organically produced. While these certification schemes typically create a premium price point, production is usually ten to 50 percent lower than that of conventional farms. Since insecticides cannot be used, some of the yield is lost to insects and other pests. Non-synthetic insecticides, such as neem extract, are permissible. Neem, like caffeine, is a naturally occurring insect repellent. It is, however, more expensive than synthetic pesticides, so most farmers only use neem on infected plants rather than broadcast spraying. Hybrid coffees are acceptable, but genetically modified coffees are not. Ironically, one genetic modification includes the insertion of the Bt gene in coffee so that it would produce a naturally occurring protein that is highly effective in reducing insect damage. The protein is normally produced in bacteria but has been used successfully in many crops without any known health effects in humans. Certified organic also prohibits synthetic fertilizers, and yield is lower in areas where the soil is not well managed. Weeds need to be controlled without using herbicides or mechanized weeding, so most weeding is done by hand, adding to labor costs. Altogether, organic coffee also tends to be more labor-intensive as farm labor has to be used rather than chemicals. This added expense can be somewhat mitigated in places that have low labor costs. Major importers of organic coffee include Holland, Germany, and the United States. Guatemala,

Kenya, and the first modern producer of organic coffee, Mexico, are three top organic producers.

For many people, coffee certification is less about the coffee itself and more about their desire for a particular social outcome connected to their purchase. As such, and for the reasons discussed above, Fair Trade, sustainable, and organic coffee tend to be of lower quality but demands a higher price. Surveys of consumer behavior have consistently shown that, in the abstract, people are willing to pay more for ethical products; however, there is a discrepancy between this attitude and actual consumer behavior as people are less willing to pay the premium for an ethical product (de Pelsmacker et al. 2005). This disconnect is likely due to some of the quality issues in ethical products and the fact that, for the most part, there is an intersection between ethical consumers and those who desire a higher quality coffee based on demographic factors such as wealth and income.

THE SOCIAL AND CULTURAL COMPONENT OF COFFEE

The production of coffee is not only important to the livelihoods and lifestyles of those who grow it, but it is also an important cultural touchstone in many coffee-growing societies. The cultural importance of coffee means that there are many myths and stories regarding how humans first noticed the invigorating effects of consuming coffee. The most famous story about how humans discovered coffee centers on Kaldi, the goat herder in Ethiopia who first noticed that the red berries of a plant he did not recognize "bewitched" and energized his goats. As the story goes, when Kaldi could not find his goats in the field he noticed that "the goats were running about, butting into each other, dancing on their hind legs and bleating excitedly . . . as he watched, one goat after another chewed off the glossy green leaves and red berries of a tree he had never seen before." (Pendergrast 2010, 21)

Although this is the most famous of the coffee origin stories, there are many similar tales from throughout East Africa and the Middle East that speak to the importance of coffee to the cultures of many people and societies. The fact that there are mythical origin stories about the emergence of coffee says a lot about the role of coffee in the countries that produce it. The story of Kaldi the goat herder should be seen as having two main elements. First, the discovery of coffee generally and how he came to notice the effects it had on his goats. Secondly, it is important that a major part of the story is the energizing effect coffee had on his goats and their behavior, since the role of caffeine has been a major part of the story of coffee from the very beginning. The invigorating effects of the caffeine contained in coffee long made government and religious authorities nervous, something that would dominate the consumption of coffee and its spread around the world, starting in the Middle Ages.

Since the origin of coffee in society can be traced to East Africa and the Middle East, much of the early spread of coffee around the world was heavily influenced by Arab and Muslim culture and traders. Since alcohol is forbidden in Muslim cultures, coffee became the default drink, and coffeehouses were the prime meeting place outside the home. "Middle Eastern society at the time did not offer nonreligious meeting places: taverns did not exist because Islam prohibited the consumption of alcoholic beverages and eating at restaurants was not customary. Therefore, coffeehouses drew people easily and facilitated a lively social atmosphere" (Tucker 2017, 53). This "lively social atmosphere" created by the consumption of coffee in coffeehouses almost immediately began to get the attention of religious and civil authorities who often considered coffee to be dangerous (it energized people!) as well as coffeehouses (energized people talking about politics!). Riots over the status of coffeehouses occurred in Cairo, Egypt, in 1521 and 1532, with opponents to the establishments coming from religious authorities but also neighbors tired of the late-night noise (Tucker 2017, 54).

One of the most notable things about the early history of coffee is the theme of coffeehouses as dangerous centers of political discourse, protest, and sometimes even revolution. Examples proliferate; however, some revolutions steeped in coffee include the American Revolution, in which coffee became a patriotic drink juxtaposed with the very British consumption of tea, and many of the ideas that pushed along the French Revolution were debated in the hundreds of Paris coffeehouses of the mid-to-late eighteenth century. The Parisian coffeehouse provided the perfect atmosphere for collecting and energizing the various aspects of French society into a revolutionary fervor. "Coffeehouses became sites for nurturing ideas of revolution as members of the upper class, including leading French thinkers, interacted with the working class" (Tucker 2017, 56–57).

Another of the central myths in the history of coffee originates in the Ottoman Empire's siege of Vienna, Austria, in 1683. When the Viennese finally repulsed the invading Ottoman Turks, the Turks supposedly fled the city so quickly that they left behind several hundred bags of coffee which were quickly identified as a valuable resource and used to start the city's first coffee shop. This story not only connects Europe to the consumption of coffee, but also to the idea that coffee, coffeehouses, and political action go together. In reality, however, the first bags of coffee to arrive in Europe in commercial quantities came through Venice, Italy, in 1740 (Jamieson 2001, 281). While the accuracy of these stories about the origin of coffee is certainly questionable, the broader point is the way in which coffee connects to the culture in the various places it is produced and consumed. "Each culture that has embraced coffee has also developed an origin myth around its introduction to the culture. Often partially factual, these myths distill the tone of a culture's relationship with the bean" (Dicum 2003, 72).

As an important coffee-producing country, Costa Rica also has a rich cafe culture with many places to enjoy a cup throughout the country. Not surprisingly, in coffee-growing regions, there are many cafes associated with either a local cooperative or coffee shops that serve as retail outlet for individual farms. Like many coffee-producing countries, many Costa Ricans in the coffee-growing regions of the country produce small amounts of coffee for their own consumption. Those who do not produce their own often purchase inexpensive coffee not suitable for export from a local grocery store or other retail outlet. As Italian-style coffee drinks and coffee that more resemble dessert become more popular around the world, Costa Ricans are at a sort of generational crossroads regarding how coffee is brewed and consumed. Since coffee was introduced to Costa Rica, it was never meant to be consumed domestically, as the vast majority of high-quality coffee was sent abroad as an important export. Due to this, coffee consumption, particularly among the older population, was more utilitarian as the vast majority of coffee consumed in-country was of lower quality. The traditional way to brew a cup of coffee in Costa Rica is to prepare the beverage in a *chorreador*—a sort of wooden frame with a fabric bag attached. The brew is similar to a pour-over style, and the brewer can make a single cup with a lot of control over the strength of the final product. Although it is very common for Costa Rican households to have modern methods of brewing coffee, such as a French press, percolator, or a chemex, the *chorreador* is seen as a cultural icon, and it is common to see the fabric bags hung out to dry on a clothesline for use the next day. The Costa Rican government has also set up health clinics and other social services for the use of migrant labor in coffee-growing regions of the country.

COFFEE LABOR IN LATIN AMERICA

Another important social aspect of the coffee industry is that the vast majority of labor used on coffee farms in Latin America is migrant labor, either migrants from other parts of the country or, in the case of Costa Rica, migrants from neighboring countries. For the most part, farm labor, such as pruning and caring for the coffee plants, is done by Nicaraguans who live permanently or semi-permanently in Costa Rica, and coffee harvesting is done by people who have migrated from Panama just for the yearly harvest. Due to the labor needs of coffee farming as well as other agricultural industries, such as bananas, Costa Rica has the highest share of migrants in its domestic population in Latin America (Voorend 2019). Among the Panamanians that migrate to harvest the coffee cherries, the largest number are from the Ngöbe Buglé cultural group, who travel as a family each season to pick coffee in Costa Rica. The Ngöbe Buglé spend the entire harvest season in Costa Rica, and much of the life of their villages in Panama is structured around migrating to Costa Rica each year for the harvest. The Ngöbe Buglé families who migrate also tend to work for the same Costa Rican families year after year—for instance, the current Ngöbe Buglé families who migrate for the harvest work for the same families their parents did, and the children, who travel with their families, will work for them as well in the future. Migrating for the harvest is so ingrained in the Ngöbe Buglé villages that their children's schools are structured around leaving for Costa Rica during the harvest season, and many other aspects of village life are determined by their migration patterns. Despite this, the Costa Rican government mandates that migrant children must attend school while in-country, and there are many small schools spread all over the coffee-growing region to serve Panamanian and Nicaraguan children.

THE POLITICAL STABILITY OF COFFEE

Due to the cultural and social centrality of coffee for much of Costa Rican history, it is not a surprise that the coffee industry would also be a central player in Costa Rican politics throughout much of its history. The story of the Costa Rican coffee industry, however, is one of a slow erosion of its power, standing and profitability across a good portion of the last century or so. Coffee has played such a pivotal role in the development of Costa Rica that Costa Ricans refer to it as "grano d'oro" (grains of gold) and reverently speak about the role of "coffee culture" in the life and history of the nation. To many Costa Ricans, "coffee culture" is much more than sitting at a cafe and enjoying a cup of coffee from a coffee-growing region such as Tarrazú or Dota; it is representative of the centrality of coffee to many Costa Ricans and to almost everyone who lives in coffee country. As such, coffee represents a window into Costa Rica's rural past and exemplifies values of family, hard work, and attention to the land. Due to this, the significance of the political, social, and economic impacts of coffee on Costa Rica cannot be overstated.

Beginning in the colonial period, Costa Rican settlers searched for an economic activity that could support them in a country covered in dense forests and rugged mountains with few easily exploitable resources. Early attempts at developing the sorts of economic activities common in other parts of Spanish colonialism proved fruitless, and the difficult terrain and distance from the center of colonial administration meant that many economic enterprises were at the mercy of pirates and other raiders, on top of the usual risks of living in the colonies. When it was discovered that coffee grew very well in many parts of the country, which roughly corresponds to the time of Costa Rican independence in the early nineteenth century, the government did all it could to encourage the cultivation of coffee in order to have an export commodity that would benefit the country. Due to this, the nineteenth century in Costa Rica is the golden age of coffee farming, and various levels of government passed laws that encouraged and in most cases privileged growing coffee for export, which helped to create the modern coffee industry in Costa Rica and a coffee elite that dominated politics for much of the time from the mid-nineteenth to early-twentieth century.

The Great Depression and its aftermath were the first major events that eroded the power of the coffee elite in Costa Rica as a slew of bureaucratic entities and new laws were created to manage the coffee industry and to curtail the power of the coffee elite. If the Great Depression started the process of curtailing the power of the coffee elite, the 1948 civil war and its aftermath dealt the biggest blow to the coffee industry via changes to tax policies that targeted coffee profits and the creation of the cooperative system. Since then, the Costa Rican government has worked feverishly to develop various industries, most prominently ecotourism and high-tech manufacturing, that have supplanted coffee as the country's chief economic engine. The next chapter will examine the development of the coffee industry in Costa Rica and in Latin America generally.

Chapter 1

Costa Rican Coffee in Regional Context

Although most of the world's highest quality coffee is grown in Latin America, coffee was originally cultivated in the Arabian Peninsula and East Africa. Coffee first arrived in Europe via the Ottoman Empire in the seventeenth century when the Turkish ambassador brought coffee beans to Paris seeking an alliance with the French (Wild 2004, 57). Once Europeans got a taste for coffee, they began looking for places it could be grown for the European market, and many of their colonies in Latin America and the Caribbean were a perfect fit due to the soil, climate, and elevation. Due to this, much of the manner in which the cultivation of coffee spread around the world, including where it is grown to this day, is due to the choices made in colonial capitals during the eighteenth century. Among the very first colonial powers to plant coffee in their colonies, the French planted coffee bushes in their Caribbean colonies starting in 1723. The British followed in 1728, planting coffee in Jamaica and Montserrat. The Portuguese planted coffee in Brazil in 1732, and the Spanish planted coffee in Cuba in 1748 (Jamieson 2001, 283). Coffee arrived in Costa Rica from Cuba in 1779, and Costa Ricans quickly discovered that coffee grew very well in the mountainous countryside of the central valley, a discovery that permanently impacted Costa Rican politics, economics and society.

Almost immediately after coffee was planted in the colonies, they began to produce large amounts to ship back to Europe, and coffee quickly became an important commodity, with Europe as its most important market. Coffee production in the colonies grew so rapidly that "before the French Revolution over 80 percent of the world's coffee production originated in European colonies in the Americas" (Topik and Samper 2006, 122). Not surprisingly, the production of a large quantity of coffee required a concomitantly large amount of farm labor, much of which came from some combination of slave, forced, and sometimes free, labor. Although coffee came to Latin America late in the period of Spanish colonialism, its cultivation and subsequent exportation all over the world, and the political, social, and economic systems it created, are still important throughout the coffee-growing countries of Latin America. As such, it is important to understand the history of coffee in the countries of Latin America, the role it played in Latin American societies, as well as the continuing legacies of coffee production. This chapter examines the introduction of the cultivation of coffee to Latin America, its history in the region, as well as its impact on the region's economies, society, and politics to this day. This chapter will also discuss the manner in which Costa Rican politics, economics and society began to develop in ways different from other coffee-growing countries in Latin America.

COLONIAL LABOR SYSTEMS AND THE SPREAD OF COFFEE

At the beginning of Spanish colonialism, labor came from the local indigenous populations, and the ability to exploit these groups as a source of labor was an important inducement for the recruitment of conquistadors. In the very earliest days of Spanish colonialism, conquistadors were motivated to go to the colonies due to their reputation for access to quick mineral wealth that could be mined by exploiting the local indigenous population for labor, which was plentiful in many parts of the colonies that also had gold and silver deposits. Later, as future generations of Spanish colonists became very powerful due to the large tracts of land they controlled in addition to a large amount of labor, the Spanish Crown needed a system that could better regulate the use of indigenous labor. Various forced labor systems were used across the colonies, most prominently, a system known as *encomienda.*

Under this system, becoming an *encomendero* (the Spanish term for those in the colonies who requested indigenous laborers from the Crown) gave conquistadors the ability to quickly amass a large amount of wealth and control over huge tracts of land. Interestingly, while the Crown granted *encomenderos* the right to indigenous labor and other forms of tribute, they did not grant them ownership of the land, which ostensibly still remained a possession of the Spanish Crown. In addition, the encomienda system should be understood as a forced labor system distinct from a slave labor arrangement, as there were a number of restrictions on what *encomenderos* could do:

> Property rights over Indian labor were restricted in three ways. First, Indians were not owned by encomenderos; they could not be bought, sold, or rented to

> others. Second, encomenderos were forbidden inheritance rights. Encomiendas did not automatically transfer to future generations. They would revert to the Crown upon the death of the second-generation encomendero, to be kept by the Crown or given to another Spaniard. Third, Indians could not be relocated from their proximate geographical area. The encomenderos were only given a right to the labor, not the land. These restrictions on trading, inheritance, and relocation distinguished Indians in encomiendas from slaves. (Yeager 1995, 843)

Part of the reason the Spaniards adopted the encomienda system was that during the reconquista of the Iberian Peninsula they used a similar system to extract labor from the conquered Moorish population. Not only was this sort of forced labor system familiar to the Spaniards, but forced labor was also familiar to much of the indigenous population who had been forced by indigenous conquerors to provide labor as tribute (Chasteen 2016, 43–44). It should also be understood that while the lives of indigenous workers improved slightly under the encomienda system due to its restrictions, the intent of the system was not to improve workers' lives but to impinge on the growing power of the conquistadors and colonists in the New World. As Spanish colonists started to build huge empires of land, slaves, and economic resources, the Spanish Crown started to think of ways to regulate their growing power.

Despite the small number of Spaniards versus the enormous number of indigenous people, the Spaniards found that the more highly centralized the indigenous population, the easier it was to graft encomienda onto the existing labor structure. It was easier still in areas that suffered from a particularly authoritarian pre-Columbian structure, a situation that created ready-made allies for the Spaniards to use in a divide and conquer strategy in their conquest of the New World. As Chasteen (2016) points out:

> Neither the Incas nor the Aztecs could have been defeated without the aid of the Spaniards indigenous allies. In Mexico, Aztec taxes and tribute had weighed heavily on the shoulders of other Nahuatl-speaking city-states. Tributary city-states had furnished sacrificial victims for the Aztec state religion. The ideology that glorified Aztec imperial expansion and bathed the pyramids of Tenochtitlan in the blood of thousands. As a result, Cortes found ready alliances. Most notably with the nearby indigenous city of Tlaxcala, an old rival of Tenochtitlan. Eager to end Aztec rule, rival cities sent thousands of warriors to help Cortes. (42)

In this way, the Spaniards were able to more quickly conquer groups like the Aztecs than they would otherwise have been able to with the difficulties in sending large numbers of Spaniards across the Atlantic Ocean. The relatively quick conquest also meant that the Spanish Crown found itself ruling over unimaginably large tracts of land and millions of people in a relatively short period of time, with very little policy in place to deal with the complexities of maintaining an empire. Due to the desire for wealth and the need for labor, the Spanish Crown encouraged the use of indigenous labor to ensure that the colonies could provide the income from tax revenue that would help to sustain the Spanish Empire and its colonies.

When Christopher Columbus landed in what would become Costa Rica on his fourth and final journey to the New World in September of 1502, he encountered many of the problems that would plague Spanish colonialism in the country for the next three centuries, such as a dense tropical rainforest filled with dangers from plants and animals as well as a small but aggressive indigenous population. Each of these problems made the Spaniards delay the colonization of Costa Rica until the mid-1550s, three decades after they were able to subdue other parts of Central America. In fact, Costa Rica got its name as an inducement for settlement as the "Rich Coast" promised infinite mineral wealth and the chance to make a fortune—a promise that repeatedly disappointed many Spaniards who went to Costa Rica with hopes of easy wealth. Since the indigenous population in Costa Rica was sparser and much more dispersed, with many being hunter-gatherers who passed through the dense tropical forests in search of game, the Spaniards also could not employ the strategies of conquest they used in other parts of the region. In this way, Costa Rica would start down a path to create social and political systems early in the colonial period that differentiated it from other countries in Latin America, many of which helped to create the stability to make Costa Rica the oldest democracy in Latin America.

Throughout Spanish colonialism, in addition to the conquistadors who were in search of easy wealth, the Spanish Crown also hoped for easy sources of wealth in its colonies. The search for land, labor, and gold became the guiding force for Spain, allowing them to extract the quinto real (Royal Fifth), which obliged the colonies to provide 20 percent of their income from conquest and mining as a tax back to Spain. Since the Spanish Crown wanted to ensure that they received the quinto real, one issue for Spain as it sent conquistadors to the New World was how to ensure they would remain loyal to the Crown once they arrived. The solution they developed was the use of a share contract between individuals going to the New World and the Spanish Crown. The Crown used the strategy of a share contract because it was the only way to ensure that Spain could recruit the number of conquistadors necessary to extract the desired amount of income from New World conquest. Under a share contract, the conquistadors (and later colonists) were required to submit the quinto real to the Spanish Crown as a sort of fee for being granted the ability to colonize the area belonging to Spain. Although not perfect, share contracts were the most palatable to the Crown because they did not require an upfront payment either from the conquistador (fixed rate contract) or the upfront payment to the *conquistador* (wage contract). The idea of a fixed rate contract was problematic because the requirement of a large payment to the Crown would have made the recruitment of conquistadors very difficult as few would have had the funds necessary to make such a large payment. Wage contracts were also a problem, as paying a *conquistador* in advance would be a large inducement for them to ignore their responsibilities to the Crown once they left Spain. Due to these issues, the Crown favored a share contract which traded partial rights to New World assets for a more efficient incentive system (Yeager 1995, 844).

The encomienda system, as well as other colonial labor practices used during the Spanish conquest, had several other important legacies for much of modern Latin America. The most important is that the strained societal relations in many countries throughout Latin America got their start in the forced labor of the colonial period, particularly the relationship between the elite and indigenous populations. This period was also the start of many elite conflicts over how the state, economy, and society should be ordered, conflicts that would come to dominate the politics of many countries in the century or so after independence from Spain. These relationships often remain strained to this day in countries with large indigenous populations and often manifest themselves in various forms of violence. Since Costa Rica had neither a large indigenous population nor many Spanish colonists, it has avoided much of the societal stress that has plagued its neighbors in the region.

The large-scale use of forced labor during the colonial period also helped to concentrate land and wealth into the hands of very few. This high concentration of land tenure has led to high economic inequality in Latin America and some of the most economically unequal countries in the world (Ferreira and Schoch 2020). Part of the reason there is such stark income and land inequality is that many of the reforms that lessened the use of indigenous labor during the colonial period were not done to make the lives of laborers any better but were instead measures that were meant to lower the power of the new colonial elite, many of whom "became much like European nobles, able to live from the labor of serf-like farmers who delivered part of their crops as regular tribute" (Chasteen 2016, 44). Despite these measures, the Spaniards were never quite able to successfully diminish the power of the wealthiest colonists, and the fault line between the Spanish Crown and the colonial elite would, a few centuries later, provide one of the major fault lines for the revolutionary movements in the region. It would also put into place a very rigid social hierarchy that in many ways remains to this day.

The tension between the Spanish Crown and the colonial elite, along with the demographic catastrophe in the indigenous population due to overwork, exploitation, and disease persuaded Spain to begin the importation of enslaved Africans. Although enslaved people had long been present in the colonies, the large-scale movement of people from Africa did not occur until after the decline of the indigenous population, culminating in the early seventeenth century. The slave trade to Latin America was so prominent that, according to historian Henry Louis Gates Jr., among the 10.7 million Africans who survived the Middle Passage and arrived in the Americas, only around 450,000 ended up in what is now the United States. This means that over 10 million went to the colonies in Latin America and the Caribbean, and almost half of those went to Brazil (PBS.org).

As the number of enslaved people imported to Brazil indicates, the slave trade was often highly concentrated, and slaves were sent in much larger numbers to places in the colonies that had "an extended plantation economy producing to supply international markets and an insufficient supply of indigenous labour" (Hensel 2007, 19). One aspect of the use of forced and slave labor is that in the example of Spanish America, the use of such labor was highly regulated from almost the moment that conquistadors arrived in the New World. In fact, the laws surrounding the use of labor, particularly slave labor, were so labyrinthine that in a royal decree in 1789 "King Carlos IV of Spain acknowledged that the legal corpus concerning colonial slavery was so vast that it had become impossible for owners and officials to know it" (de la Fuente and Gross 2010, 470). The combination of forced labor systems such as encomienda (among many) and the later use of African slaves on a large-scale impacted the modern labor systems of the majority of states in Latin America.

It is also important to note the long-term continuity of the labor systems of much of Spanish America and Brazil across multiple time periods and different ruling groups. This continuity exists because the most highly centralized of the pre-Columbian groups exacted a large amount of tribute from subject peoples before the arrival of the Spaniards, a system that made it easy for the Spaniards to co-opt when they began to colonize the Americas. When Latin America and Brazil began to declare independence in the first couple of decades of the nineteenth century, the old colonial elite, most of whom were also the revolutionary leaders, were able to continue with many of the labor practices put in place during colonialism. Due to this, and despite the adoption of modern labor standards in the countries of Latin America, many practices rooted in the past five centuries of the relationship between labor and the elite remain as vestiges of the colonial period.

Part of the reason that Costa Rica developed differently from many of its neighbors in Central America is that without a large indigenous population, the colonial legacies experienced by other parts of Latin America are not as acute. In addition, Costa Rica was so unprofitable for Spain that the few Spanish authorities who were sent there during the colonial era (and that number was small) obeyed the orders from Spain, which meant that

Costa Rica was essentially ungoverned by Spanish colonialism (Vogt 2019, 13–14). While many scholars and tourists, as well as some Costa Ricans, idealize Costa Rica as some sort of Switzerland of Central America (a slogan once used by the Costa Rican Tourism Authority), it should be noted that the historical difference between Costa Rican development and places like Guatemala, El Salvador, or Nicaragua starts in the time of Spanish colonialism and specifically the labor system created by the large number of Spanish colonists sent there to turn a profit for the Crown. In many ways, the most important difference between modern Costa Rica and a country like modern Guatemala is the history of wage labor in Costa Rica and slave labor in Guatemala and the sum total of these systems over five centuries and how they affected societal relations.

ECONOMIC THEORY AND SPANISH COLONIALISM

Similarly to its colonial competitors, Spain's actions in its colonies can be explained by the era's prevailing mercantilist ideology. Mercantilism, broadly construed, argues that wealth and power come from positive trade balances and protected markets. As such, Spain's colonies in the Americas were seen as a source of low-cost raw materials and as a protected market to sell finished goods since everything purchased in the colonies had to originate in Spain. In this way, mercantilism seeks to enrich the power of the state through the use of commerce with a direct connection between the accumulation of wealth and the ability to exercise power. Juxtaposed to a system of globalization, the theory behind mercantilism is that international trade is a zero-sum game creating only winners and losers, and not the positive-sum game espoused by neoliberal economists today. In addition, mercantilism dictated that the accumulation of territory not only added positively to the balance sheet of a state, but also that denying it to a competitor provided a secondary benefit.

Most scholars trace the origin of mercantilism to Jean-Baptiste Colbert, who served as Finance Minister during the reign of Louis XIV of France. Colbert saw the state as the center of economic life and sought ways to enrich it in order to expand its power. These ideas fit perfectly with the rule of Louis XIV, the Sun King around which the rest of France and the world orbited. One key difference between Colbert's vision of mercantilism (known as Colbertism) and the sort of mercantilism practiced in Spain is that Colbert was much more focused on manufacturing and put far less emphasis on the economic pursuits the Spaniards valued such as the mining of precious metals. Colbert himself noted this when he said, "Fashion is to France what gold mines are to the Spaniards" (Mikosch 1990, 112). In this way, the sort of mercantilism practiced by the Spaniards differed from that of other European countries such as France and England.

The Spaniards were so fixated on the pursuit of precious metals because of their use as currency since ancient times and their relative scarcity in Western Europe. "The absence of adequate natural gold deposits in Western Europe conditioned the frequent association of gold with the rare, exotic, foreign, and distant. Generations before the first voyage of Columbus, gold's desirability and high value were encoded into narratives emphasizing its remoteness, inaccessibility, and alien origins. While scarce in Europe, gold was held to be amply available elsewhere, to 'the other' or in the lands of the other, to beings from faraway places, cultures, and latitudes ancient and medieval European sailors, travelers, and travel writers encountered in their real and imaginary forays overseas" (Estow 1993, 88). This pursuit of tangible economic assets, including labor and natural resources in addition to precious metals, put the Crown on a downward trajectory that no amount of wealth or reform to the system could help to remedy. In many ways, the power of Spain was on a downward trend starting from the earliest days of the conquest, so much so that even many contemporary colonial competitors saw the errors in the Spaniards' plans:

> To European observers of the seventeenth and eighteenth centuries, the Spanish empire had become a model of what not to do. Although early generations of British and French explorers in the Americas sought to emulate the pursuit of Indian gold, the political theorists of Spain's rivals soon shunned what they perceived to be the fundamental errors of its expansion and governance. Obsessed with land-based conquest and rule over indigenous peoples, so the critique went, the Spanish had utterly neglected commerce. This fatal flaw was seen as the cause of its perceived ruin. (Schneider 2015, 3)

The connection between mercantilism and land rather than commerce was another factor that helped to create the extreme concentration of wealth seen to this day throughout Latin America. Since the Spanish Crown used land as an inducement to settle the New World, this set in motion a series of events that would lead to a modern elite in many Latin American countries who can trace their lineage back to an original conquistador. This means that many of the descendants of the original elites who came to the New World still control that same land over five centuries later. The nature of the share contract and the distance from Spain, not to mention Spain's strong desire to get their quinto real, meant that commerce was often neglected as the individual colonists could control far more resources with dominion over land. Conversely, under English mercantilism, the colonial state was the principal actor rather than the individual colonial elites.

> The (English colonial) state carefully controlled land distribution and the pace of settlement, including by regulating minimum and maximum acreages and by setting land prices. Land policies in turn reinforced the prevalence of smallholders and prevented the formation of powerful landed elites with the capacity to establish monopolistic structures harmful to long-run economic development. Moreover, the land policies in British settlement colonies facilitated economic transactions among farmers and planters. (Lange, Mahoney and vom Hau 2006, 1442)

When coffee started to be produced in Latin America, one of the manifestations of Spain neglecting commerce in the coffee trade during the colonial period is that other countries took the lead in the burgeoning coffee industry and enjoyed the broader economic benefits of reexporting it to other countries. In this way, the British became the central hub of coffee from the colonies that was reexported, mostly to Europe. The re-exportation phase of the coffee trade continued to center on London, but the data reveal the emergence of a significant reexport trade possessing two notable features. First, in contrast to tea, reexported coffee was dispatched to outlets outside the protected markets of Ireland and the American colonies. Second, unlike tobacco at this time, coffee was reshipped directly to its principal market in the German territories without passing through the entrepot, Amsterdam (Smith 1996, 185).

Contrary to other countries in the region, one of the most important factors in the historical development of Costa Rica was its isolation from most of the colonial administration, which was headquartered in present-day Guatemala. This isolation from Spanish colonialism meant that Costa Rica developed differently from the rest of the region and, in many ways, was much more autonomous than other parts of Spanish colonialism, which often fell under a more direct form of colonial rule. In fact, "(Costa Rica) was officially ignored by the colonial government, since trade was prohibited through the Atlantic Coast: colonial law required that all imports come from Spain by way of Guatemala" (Jones 1990, 23). The isolation from colonial authorities and lack of access to easy wealth meant that Costa Rica never had a large number of Spanish colonists. In fact, the 1611 census shows only 330 Spaniards, and in 1700 the number had risen to 2,146; however, this number also includes children of colonists who were born in Costa Rica (Booth 1998, 33).

In this way, Costa Rica was not only socially and politically isolated, but the prohibition on trade from its Atlantic Coast also made Costa Rica economically isolated as well. This isolation further manifested itself by discouraging Spanish colonists from settling there, which diminished Costa Rica's political clout. In fact, while some wealthy colonists did migrate to Costa Rica, the economic difficulties and lack of any easy access to wealth meant that they lived a much more modest lifestyle than the elites in other

Spanish colonies (Booth 1998, 33). Another difference between Costa Rica and its neighbors was the relatively small number of indigenous groups encountered by early settlers. These numbers were further reduced via exposure to disease and overwork, as in other areas of Spanish colonization, and by the mid-eighteenth century, the indigenous population was almost totally decimated. The threat was seen as so small to the Spanish authorities that in 1677 they shifted the budget from fighting indigenous groups to fighting English raiders and pirates, especially on the Caribbean coast (Quirós 2004, 21).

The small number of indigenous groups in Costa Rica meant that Costa Rica would not establish the sort of societal relations that have plagued countries such as Guatemala or El Salvador, with large indigenous populations. Without an easily accessible indigenous labor force to exploit, Costa Rica developed a labor system that differed significantly from its neighbors. The development of a labor system that is different from its neighbors began early in the colonial period since "the Spaniards never discovered any mineral resources of commercial value. Nor did Costa Rica contain a large native labor force to produce exotic tropical crops for export to Europe . . . the conquistadores in the interior of Costa Rica were reduced by the 1560s to pillaging the natives' crops and were soon obliged to take up farming themselves" (Hall 1985, 72). After the mid-sixteenth century, there was very little inducement for conquistadors to go to Costa Rica as sources of quick wealth (mineral resources and slaves) were in short supply. This situation is in sharp juxtaposition to former colonies such as Perú, in which a large indigenous population and a significant amount of mineral wealth meant much easier access to large amounts of wealth and a persistent legacy of economic inequality and exploitation. For instance, Dell (2010) found that the legacy of the mit'a forced labor system in Perú has had a lasting effect across Peruvian society and estimated that in modern Perú it lowered household consumption by 25 percent, affected child development, land tenure, the dispersal and use of public goods, and market participation (1899). Given its colonial experience, Costa Rica was spared from many of the societal problems that plague Perú and the other modern Latin American states.

Costa Rica was not, of course, the only place where Spaniards were disappointed in the lack of easy access to wealth, but the reputation of Costa Rica as a place where you needed to work hard to scratch out a living from the earth without the inducement of the possibility for wealth based on either mining or human exploitation attracted a different type of colonist. "In the second half of the sixteenth century, for example, (Costa Rica was) described as 'the poorest and most miserable in all the Americas', so that the Spanish governor had to till his own land to survive" (Augelli 1987, 2). This difference then perpetuated itself through Costa Rican history to the modern differences seen between it and its neighbors. In Costa Rica, with little available labor, it was necessary for a wage labor system to develop in order for Costa Rica to meet its production needs. In many ways, the development trajectories of Costa Rica and places like Perú are starkly different because of five centuries of wage labor in Costa Rica and five centuries of slave/forced labor in Perú. As Ameringer (1982) points out, Costa Rican societal relations were exceptional because juxtaposed to many countries in the region, "(labor) was not made up of a conquered race or a of imported slaves held in inferior status but the institutionalized tyranny of a ruling class, but of persons accustomed to being free and who had the same cultural heritage of the emerging coffee barons" (3).

COFFEE AND POWER IN POSTCOLONIAL LATIN AMERICA

In many places in Latin America, the introduction of coffee during the colonial period helped to create and maintain the power and wealth of the landed coffee elite in the postrevolutionary period. "When the tides of decolonization began to sweep through the European tropical colonies, beginning with South America in the nineteenth century, these economic inequalities were maintained, and often further institutionalized" (Dicum 2003, 73). This is because, for the most part, the colonial elite were able to maintain their power over society based in large part in coffee-growing countries on the economic power that came from the cultivation of coffee and the accumulation of vast tracts of land. Here again, Costa Rica took a different path, as Vogt (2019) points out:

> The concentration of Costa Rican land was smaller in comparison with the rest of Central America. While in Guatemala and El Salvador, coffee production revolved around the hacienda, the large property, in Costa Rica, coffee was planted in small and medium-sized land. Despite the social stratification that came from the colony, small and medium property was the rule in Costa Rica. An elite linked to coffee activity was not therefore like the great Guatemalan proprietors who relied on forced first nation labor. Nor the Salvadoran expropriating first nation communal lands, making of these a peasant without semiproletarian land. (19)

The coffee elite in many parts of Latin America was able to parlay the economic and social power built during the colonial period into political power. A number of countries' national leaders, particularly in Central America, were either coffee growers themselves or had ties to the coffee industry. As a result, much of the nineteenth century in Latin America was a battle among elites with differing visions of how the various national political systems should be structured. Once they gained power, they often protected their newly consolidated power via the construction of an authoritarian regime enforced by the national military.

This struggle over the structure of political systems was roughly divided into two camps: those that were in favor of a more democratic structure (liberals) and those who wanted to continue with a political structure more similar to the Spaniards (conservatives). There were many regional variations, and the colonial experiences of individual states helped to create the postcolonial political, economic and social structures. However, for the most part, the colonial elite were not only able to hang on to their power, but in many places and in many ways, they were able to expand it.

The nineteenth century in Latin America is replete with stories about the so-called "man on horseback" who used his personal charisma and force of arms to gain power, only to be deposed soon thereafter by someone else. The instability of many nineteenth-century Latin American national governments motivated leaders to begin the process of constitutionalizing their political power around a more legalistic basis. The outcome of this was that many Latin American national constitutions were written in a way that did little to limit the power of the chief executive and, in fact, usually expanded far beyond the sort of limited government constitutionalism we see in the United States. This, in turn, laid the foundation for the use of government power by elites to control the economic system and to ensure that political opposition was held to a minimum. This often meant that groups like coffee workers were encouraged, at the point of a gun, to show up to work every day. According to Loveman (1993, 375), "the most favored constitutional instruments for confronting political opposition were regimes of exception. These included the delegation of extraordinary powers to executives and other officials, suspension of civil liberties and rights, and constitutional dictatorship." Despite the rapid change in many national constitutions in the region, the legacy of a powerful chief executive persists in the majority of Latin American states. Furthermore, these powerful chief executives often presided over a coercive and sometimes violent state apparatus. In Central America, for instance, "the dispersion of destructive power throughout the nineteenth century gave birth to states that achieved remarkable success, by the second third of the twentieth century, in consolidating and deploying fairly unified instruments of coercion" (Holden 1996, 438).

In Costa Rica, due to the relatively small population, lack of economic resources, and the wide availability of land, the "emergent coffee grower elite that dominated politics never adopted the military-guaranteed labor schemes employed elsewhere in Central America" (Booth 1998, 36). In fact, at no time in Costa Rican history prior to its total abolishment in 1949 was the Costa Rican military an important part of society. This meant that Costa Rica developed a wage labor rather than a forced labor system, which in turn created a more differentiated social system that gave birth to competing social interests. In other Central American countries, there was a very small but very wealthy elite that was able to dictate the terms of the political, economic and social systems based on their overwhelming influence over society. Since Costa Rica was much more economically differentiated, the early national development of the nineteenth century created a much more pluralistic society.

In a stark but mostly symbolic difference between itself and its neighbors, Costa Rica never developed a presidential residence. When someone is elected as the President of Costa Rica, they need to purchase or rent someplace to live in San José if they do not already have one. In addition, Costa Rica does not provide an official car or airplane. There is a Casa Presidencia in San Jose; however, it is used as government offices, and staff joke about living there (*Tico Times* 2014). Costa Rica never developed a presidential residence because, in the nineteenth century, the president was expected to spend a portion of time in each of the four quadrants of Costa Rica to better understand what was happening in each of them rather than spending most of their time in San Jose.

The power of the coffee elite throughout Latin America was further expanded by the enormous growth of coffee production and consumption in the century or so after independence from Spain. During this period, the worldwide trade in coffee expanded dramatically from 320 metric tons in 1770, to 90,000 metric tons in 1820, 450,000 metric tons in 1870, to 1,600,000 metric tons in 1920. At the same time, per capita consumption of coffee in the United States, which has always been one of the primary markets for Latin American coffee since independence, went from 3 pounds in 1830, to 10 pounds in 1900, to 16 pounds in 1960 (Roseberry 1991, 353). This level of per capita coffee consumption has remained fairly stable in the United States over the last several decades; however, the average number of cups consumed has increased, mostly due to the popularity of Italian-style coffee, which uses small amounts of coffee to produce. This expansion of consumption, with its concurrent increase in production, helped to transform the farms in many Latin American countries and plantations of the elite from subsistence to large-scale operations.

As the coffee industry grew, the coffee elite could no longer simply rely on the two main economic engines of colonialism, land and labor, which they had been able to exploit even after colonialism was officially over. As the coffee industry became more complex, the coffee elite began to see a shortage of technical expertise in the coffee industry, particularly in the areas of processing and finance as their businesses expanded. Beginning in the mid-to-late nineteenth century, the coffee elite turned to European immigration to fill some of the gaps in technical expertise in their coffee operations. "The new immigrants generally used their skills to move into the more technical and financially demanding. But also more profitable processing and export activities" (Paige 1997, 15). The influx of European immigrants into the processing and exporting side of the business meant that they often controlled the most profitable parts of the business, while the coffee elite, still often in control of large tracts of land, found themselves engaged in the much less profitable production end of the coffee business. Of course, the shrewder coffee elites found a way to combine their control of land and labor with the technical skills of recent European immigrants. "(The new European immigrants) married into the local gentry and were assimilated into the Hispanic elite" (Paige 1997, 15). Not surprisingly, the more aspects of the coffee business that could be consolidated into a single operation, the more money could be made. This means that in a lot of Latin America, during the nineteenth century, many members of the coffee elite tried to expand their operations from coffee cultivation to as many other aspects of the business as possible, such as shipping and exporting.

While Costa Rica has also consistently had a labor shortage throughout its history, it has relied much more on migrant labor for the coffee fields and did not actively recruit European immigrants in the way that states such as Argentina had done. The only caveat to that is that Costa Rica did recruit people from the Caribbean, mostly Jamaica, to work in the banana fields on the Caribbean side of the country. In general, however, the labor shortage in Costa Rica meant that farmers there needed to pay workers for their labor, and since the vast majority were migrants (this is the case to this day), they could decide whether or not to migrate to Costa Rica each year, something that encouraged the Costa Rican government and the coffee industry to pay these workers at levels that would ensure their return each year.

In other parts of Latin America, the creation of a coffee elite made up of Latin American landowners and newly arrived European immigrants, while relatively rare, helped to create a landed coffee class that dominated the politics of many countries of Latin America for decades. Despite the importance of attracting European immigrants with technical and financial skills, most immigration from Europe to Latin America was for farm labor, much of which was actively recruited. While many countries in Latin America actively recruited European immigrants, Brazil did so very aggressively:

> The state engaged in a remarkable coordination of planter needs and labor supply. Immigrants would be transferred from Santos to a hostel in Sao

> Paulo, where the state would serve as labor contractor. While at the hostel, the immigrant family would sign a contract to work on a particular plantation and would then be given railroad passage from Sao Paulo to the interior. (Roseberry 1991, 364)

These recruitment practices meant that by the early twentieth century, practically all control of the coffee industry was either in the hands of traditional Latin American elite families or European immigrants or, in the case of intermarriage, both. As a result, coffee elite families of nonaristocratic or nonimmigrant backgrounds are rare in Latin America (Paige 1997, 18). This served to further exacerbate the problems of wealth and income inequality and further solidified a social hierarchy in much of Latin America that in many cases still controls the coffee industry to this day. Furthermore, the hold that large producers had over every aspect of the coffee supply chain made it exceedingly difficult for smaller operations to break into the market.

THE GOLDEN AGE OF COFFEE PRODUCTION

The latter part of the nineteenth century through the time of the Great Depression was the golden age for coffee production in Latin America as demand for the (now) daily staple as well as other goods from the region skyrocketed. Even with the importance of other export products, coffee had a remarkable ascent to prominence as its production expanded twentyfold during the nineteenth century (Topik 2004, 1). This led to growth in the middle class as Latin American economies consolidated the gains of integration into the world economy into significant economic growth in the coffee industry as well as the broader economy. In addition, this era saw an enormous uptick in foreign direct investment and technological innovations based on integration into the world market. The new states in Latin America meant new markets and new possibilities for investment. The increase in outside investment into Latin American economies represented a fundamental shift from the region's long colonial history of dealing almost exclusively with Spain and Portugal to new relationships with Great Britain and the United States. Not surprisingly, the British were one of the first to jump at these new opportunities; "there was a marked renewal of interest in Latin America by the London capital market with the flotation of new government issues and the commencement of railroad investment" (Stone 1977, 692). This interest translated into a great deal of investment, including an increasing amount from private investors rather than the UK government. From an investment of £81 million in 1865, the British presence in Latin America grew to £1.2 trillion in 1913 with ever-increasing amounts provided by private investors (Stone 1977, 692). Especially important for the growth of coffee exports was the expansion of railroad systems across a handful of Latin American countries. "The railroad meant that the quality of coffee was better, and more importantly, cheaper, more fertile lands were now accessible in the interior" (Topik 2004, 21). The United States also found an interest in coffee and was the only major market to import coffee tax-free, which combined with a fifteenfold increase in its population meant that by the end of the nineteenth century the United States was importing around 40 percent of the world's coffee (Topik 2004, 24).

This era also saw the rise of a nascent working class as workers in sectors that supported export industries understood their importance to the national economy, which led to a surge of labor mobilization (Skidmore and Smith 2005, 49). The combination of outside investment, production and export increases, along with rising profits, meant that elites in many countries tolerated labor mobilization as the workforce had shown itself to be relatively stable and willing to show up to work, although the effects of the Great Depression and later the Cold War would change this attitude precipitously. It should also be mentioned that the influx of workers from Europe in the years between 1880 and 1920 also helped to push along the labor movement as they carried with them some of the political thought of the working class percolating at the time in many European countries.

In total, the golden age of coffee in Latin America saw a significant increase in the production and consumption of coffee and the concentration of wealth among many of the traditional coffee elites whose power was enhanced by the arrival (and sometimes active recruitment) of European immigrants. In many countries, this would mean the ascension of a small number of coffee-growing family dynasties into very large operations that dominated the economies, politics, and society of their home countries. Despite these phenomena, many countries experienced a significant amount of growth due to the export of coffee and other agricultural products. However, this growth would be upended by the Great Depression, which would devastate the economic systems of Latin America and hit many coffee farmers especially hard.

THE DEVELOPMENT OF COFFEE IN COSTA RICA IN THE EARLY NATIONAL PERIOD

With the growing popularity of coffee in Europe and the possibility of a viable export market, the Costa Rican government strongly encouraged the cultivation of coffee plants soon after independence. "Costa Rica's local governments, and later the national government, encouraged (coffee) cultivation in hopes of a new source of prosperity. They gave plants to the poor, decreed that every homeowner plant a few trees near his or her house, exempted growers from tithes, and offered free land to anyone that would plant coffee on it" (Hiltunen Biesanz et al. 1999, 21). Between the ease with which coffee grew in many parts of the country and the manner in which the government privileged its cultivation, the nineteenth century saw the rise of coffee as an export crop, and it was the beginning of a golden age in the cultivation of coffee.

Costa Rica's isolated position from Spanish colonialism and its high level of poverty meant that, with independence the new government immediately began looking for sources of revenue. In fact, Costa Rican would-be elites spent much of the colonial period in search of some sort of moneymaking resource that could help them climb the social ladder, but were hampered by Spanish policy that allowed for very little of their own economic development. With practically no gold, a small indigenous population, and failed attempts to create cacao and then tobacco industries, coffee must have seemed like the answer to their prayers. The early success of coffee and the relative ease with which it would grow in several regions of the country made it a logical choice for an export crop that generations of colonists had sought. Soon after Costa Rican independence, "in 1821, the town council of San José passed a decree providing free state land and free coffee seedlings to any individual who agreed to plant them. This resolution was followed by a similar one from the councils of Cartago and La Unión in the same year, requiring all of the families within their jurisdiction to plant from twenty to twenty-five coffee bushes in their backyards" (Seligson 1980, 15). With these declarations, coffee would inhabit a privileged place in Costa Rican society as the government passed a number of laws starting in 1821 that encouraged coffee cultivation and put it at the center of the economy. These included exempting coffee from the payment of the 10 percent ecclesiastical tax paid to the church, a decree that stated anyone growing coffee on public land assumed ownership of that land, and several government decrees to plant coffee in several parts of the country. Given these efforts, it would take from 1821 until 1832 for Costa Rica to grow enough coffee to export (Seligson 1980, 15).

As in much of Latin America, transport was a major problem for Costa Rican coffee farmers in the early national period as the Spaniards built very little infrastructure, making shipping very difficult. Given the fact that Spain put very few resources into Costa Rica, compared to other parts of the colonies, the infrastructure there was even worse. Given that Costa Rica still ranks relatively poorly on many measures of infrastructure development, it is hard to imagine the difficulties in travel during the mid-nineteenth century. With these difficulties in mind, most coffee in this early period was shipped by ox cart (elaborately painted ox carts are a cultural symbol of Costa Rica to this day), and the dense forest and mountainous terrain made these trips even more difficult. For instance, Cerro de la Muerte, south of San José, is famous among Costa Ricans as the "Mountain of Death" due to the difficulty in shipping goods via ox cart and the number of people who perished trying to do so. One way that Costa Rica dealt with these difficulties was to ship its coffee to Chile via Panama, where it was mixed with inferior quality Chilean coffee and repackaged as Café Chileno de Valparaíso for the European market (Seligson 1980, 15). Shipping through an intermediary meant that Costa Rican coffee farmers received only a portion of the profits from their coffee, and mixing it with inferior coffee beans marked as another country's coffee did not provide a marketing boost for true Costa Rican coffee.

Costa Rica's "big break" came in 1843 when English Captain William Le Lacheur sailed into Puntarenas harbor and found coffee growers willing to trust him to sell their coffee in Europe. Two years later he returned with payment for the shipment and began a flourishing coffee trade between England and Costa Rica (Hiltunen Biesanz et al. 1999, 21). The newly flourishing trade in coffee meant that it was the most important export in Costa Rica from the mid-nineteenth to the mid-twentieth century. As coffee became more and more popular in Europe, it was by far Costa Rica's most important export for the second half of the nineteenth century due in large part to its advantage of being a (virtually) nonperishable commodity that could be shipped via ox cart in the absence of more modern transportation systems (Hall 1985, 74–75).

Costa Rica capitalized on the growing demand for coffee early in its history due to a relatively stable political and social system and the fact that the coffee industry was based (mostly) on small-scale producers and wage labor, in contrast to many of its neighbors in the region. Writing in 1897, George Earl Church traveled to Costa Rica and found:

> A peasant proprietor class, consisting of hard-working sturdy farmers, who are owners of little areas of coffee plantations, or of carts and oxen engaged in internal trade. This class gives to the country most of its political stability. Wealth is more generally distributed than in any other Spanish-American state, and the taxes are very light. These might readily be doubled without any hardship to the people. The mental, moral, and material advancement which Costa Rica has made since it emerged from the baneful shadow of Spain is remarkable. (Church, 1879, 79)

That is not to say that Costa Rica, by the end of the nineteenth century, did not have an upper class of coffee farmers who were able to grow wealthy due to coffee exports or that Costa Rica was a democratic country in the modern sense, but that the nature of that elite was different from other countries in the region. As Bell (1971) argues, "most families lived isolated one from the other and earned a rather sparse living by their own work on their own land. There were those who prospered more than others, but in general, a sense of equality and frugality reigned" (5). This sense of equality was present in 1889 when Costa Rica held what is widely considered to be its first completely free and fair election for president in the country. Prior to this, "throughout much of the nineteenth century, however, literacy and property ownership requirements and the exclusion of women barred all but about 10 percent of the citizenry from voting. Most elections were indirect. Those with the franchise voted only in the first round of elections to choose electors (usually from the coffee aristocracy) who in turn would choose the actual officeholders" (Booth 1987, 44). The "Generation of 1889," as it came to be known, would lay the groundwork for Costa Rican democracy and saw the construction of several large infrastructure projects, including Costa Rica's railroad (completed in 1910) and the national theater in San José (completed in 1897). The national theater in particular is seen as a testament to the success of coffee exports in the nineteenth century and is a treasured Costa Rican institution. The national theater is also an interesting example of the attempts in Latin America generally to attract European immigrants. While the theater was constructed in order to show off the wealth of the Costa Rican coffee industry, it was also built to serve as an advertisement that there was classic European-style culture in Costa Rica for any Europeans who may want to immigrate. It also is an interesting combination of European motifs, such as a statue of Ludwig von Beethoven, and the ceiling of the theater itself is decorated with images of coffee and bananas, an homage to Costa Rican agriculture and those who built it.

The Generation of 1889 and the politics of the late nineteenth century would also help to solidify the progressive nature of the coffee elite and their desire, broadly construed, to create a pacific democracy in which all Costa Ricans can reap the rewards of a stable and democratic country. They also initiated several large-scale building projects, including the construction of a national railroad to assist in the exportation of coffee, funded by loans from English banks. As these loans became more difficult for the government to repay, in 1893 the Costa Rican government increased taxes on coffee and declared, "Notwithstanding the desires of the Government to protect the agriculture of the country in order that it may reach its greatest development, in the present circumstances, although accidentally, it is necessary to ask of it the resources that the Nation needs" (Oficina de Café from Seligson 1977, 221). This marked the beginning of the idea that coffee profits could be used for national development, a phenomenon that would dominate the relationship between the government and the coffee industry to the current day. This was also the beginning of the idea that the Costa Rican government used coffee profits as a source of government revenue, but it certainly would not be the last.

Despite attempts to consolidate democracy and a deeply ingrained pacific tradition, Costa Rica experienced its first major deviation from democratic norms since the 1889 election on January 27, 1917, when President Alfredo González Flores, attempting to run for a second term despite the constitutional prohibition on reelection, was deposed in a coup d'etat by brothers Federico and Joaquin Tinoco. Federico assumed the presidency in a quickly called election in which he was the only candidate (Hiltunen Biesanz et. al. 1999, 27). The Tinoco brothers were initially popular due to angst over González's attempt to run for a second term, as well as their opposition to some of the taxes imposed by his administration. Despite this, Tinoco was driven from office on August 13, 1919, by an uprising against his usurpation of power after he introduced bills to restart the death penalty and eliminate the direct vote, as "Costa Ricans might have tolerated an ineffective government, but they repudiated one that restricted liberties they had come to expect" (Hiltunen Biesanz et. al. 1999, 27). Government instability continued when the next president, Juan Quirós Segura, vice president under Tinoco, served in that capacity for a little more than two weeks until he was forced to resign by Washington, which did not recognize his government as legitimate. Next was the eight-month interim presidency of Francisco Aguilar Barquero, who would serve until the election of Julio Acosta García in 1920. Acosta García's short-term in office belied his important role in getting Costa Rican democracy back on track.

Despite the success with which the Generation of 1889 was able to cultivate a democratic ethic that differentiated Costa Rica from its neighbors, by the 1920s and 1930s the movement started to run out of steam. As Rosenberg (1979) points out, "as social problems mounted in the 1920s and 1930s, their nineteenth-century ideological frame of reference largely inhibited them from considering innovative state-sponsored social policy" (118). These social problems, such as poverty and lack of access to land and education, among many others, provided a perfect template for the rise of left-wing politics in Costa Rica, with the Costa Rican Communist Party at its forefront as "the banner of modernization and reform passed from the Reform Party of the 1920s to the Communist Party" (Bell 1971, 11). The 1920s and 1930s contributed a great deal to the trajectory of Costa Rica and the manner in which an inherently conservative and agrarian-based Roman Catholic country could adopt many of the ideas of its homegrown Communist Party while remaining pro-American and anti-communist.

Given the manner in which Costa Rica experienced colonialism, the development of coffee as an export industry also took a different path from that of its neighbors. The coffee boom of the nineteenth century "created a growing class of yeoman farmers who could live decently, producing coffee with family labor. The large yeomanry. the absence of Indians, and the abolition of slavery in 1821 kept the agricultural labor supply scarce and wages high during much of the nineteenth century" (Booth, 1998, 36). The scarcity and concurrent high cost of labor in Costa Rica also meant that the development of coffee in nineteenth-century Costa Rica was on a smaller scale and with considerably less wealth concentration than other Latin American coffee-producing societies because coffee farmers had to pay additional costs for labor that could have otherwise been spent on expanding their operations and concentrating their wealth. In coffee-producing countries with a surplus of labor that led to lower labor costs, the coffee elite were much more able to use the extra money to dominate that country's coffee production.

Another legacy of Spanish colonialism is that, given the very low number of settlers to Costa Rica (just a few thousand for the entire colonial period from 1502–1821) (Hall 1985, 51), land was abundant. In Costa Rica, "land was viewed as essentially limitless in supply, while the demand for it made by the tiny colonial population was almost nonexistent. As a result, there was simply no market for agricultural land and possession was denied to no one" (Seligson 1980, 8–9). In totality, the experience of Costa Rica during the colonial period is one of few settlers, very little forced labor, or easily extractable resources, which meant that most people were poor but with easy access to land. These situations vary considerably from the regional norm and have marked Costa Rica as different from the beginning. In particular, the abundance of available land rather than land scarcity is particularly noteworthy. This abundance of land in Costa Rica had a number of consequences for national development:

> The colonial frontier experience in Costa Rica gave rise to certain traits that continued and intensified later. Chief among them were the perception of abundant, almost limitless land; a wasteful mentality toward soil, forests, and other resources; large families to provide farm labor, land tenure structured primarily on smallholdings; a strong farming as a way of life and limited association with cities; slash-and-burn agricultural practices that placed little emphasis on conservation, or use of fertilizers and that required comparatively large amounts of land to remain viable; and assumptions that land was free or cheap and that any campesino had the right to as much as he needed to support his family. (Augelli 1987, 5)

Given the differences in historical trajectory between Costa Rica and countries such as Guatemala, the colonial period in Guatemala provides a template for societal conflict, which was exacerbated when coffee became a major export in the nineteenth century. As Paige (1997) argues,

> The Guatemalan elite, particularly in its national sector, was characterized by large estate, large amounts of land under estate control, and large numbers of people under tight seigniorial restrictions. The most striking contrast with the Guatemalan elite was that of Costa Rica, in which the agrarian faction was relatively weakly developed because it lost control over substantial amounts of land to a persistent class of family farmers. (86–87)

Due to these social differences, one of the primary ways that the Costa Rican colonial experience deviated from much of the region is that Costa Rica was not particularly attractive to potential conquistadors and had relatively few indigenous peoples. In addition, Costa Rica never experienced the violent upheaval associated with the conquest. As a result, Costa Rica does not have the legacy of colonial labor practices that are seen in other parts of Latin America. This not only spared Costa Rica from the violence of the Spanish conquest but also helped to create the idea among Costa Ricans that they have built a more peaceful country in which collaboration and cooperation are the norm. In fact, postcolonial Costa Rican political leaders used this notion as a way to frame postcolonial development. "The Costa Ricans' frame upheld as truth the claim that they were, both by reputation and in fact, an inherently peaceable and diligent people. This frame, in turn, restricted the intensity and scope of political debate and struggle, creating in the process sufficient space for intra-elite consensus building and, ultimately, the political stability necessary to craft and execute developmental policies" (Cruz 2000, 278).

Chapter 2

The Modern Costa Rican Coffee Industry

Coffee has long been central to understanding the politics, economics, and society of Costa Rica. This chapter will provide an analysis of the role of coffee in modern Costa Rica, focusing on its role of coffee as an agricultural export and its impact on the Costa Rican economy, politics, and broader society. This chapter will also examine how and why the coffee industry has changed over the course of Costa Rica's history and how those changes have affected the people who depend on the cultivation of coffee for their livelihood. The story of the coffee industry in Costa Rica is one of declining power within the overall economy over time as elected officials have tried to minimize the role of coffee as a prominent export. The change in the role of coffee in Costa Rican exports began after the Great Depression to set up the current social democratic system, and the government has since further diminished coffee's power as it has feverishly pursued economic development that has relegated the exportation of coffee to the background.

LATIN AMERICA REACTS TO THE GREAT DEPRESSION

The early effects of the Great Depression in Latin America centered on the way national economies depended on the export of primary goods, often a single commodity, to U.S. and European markets. In addition, the extent to which many Latin American countries were dependent on outside capital caused a lot of additional economic damage as investment from outside the region slowed to a trickle. Across the region, the governments of Latin America responded to these events in similar ways, such as halting gold shipments, devaluing their currencies, and defaulting on their foreign debts (Twomey 1983, 241). Region-wide economic problems were further exacerbated when the demand for coffee during the early years of the Great Depression fell precipitously. This created a panic among many coffee-growing countries and led to such extreme measures as Brazil destroying around 80 percent of the world's coffee supply due to low prices. Due to the extremely low demand for coffee and several years of overproduction, the Brazilian government actively purchased domestically produced coffee and destroyed it in an effort to lower world supply in hopes of boosting its price. To lower the national coffee supply, from 1931 to 1944 the Brazilian government destroyed 26.96 percent of its coffee stocks, including 1937 in which a shocking 70.62 percent of its coffee inventory was destroyed (Astorino 2012).

Schemes specific to boosting the price of coffee through government purchases (and subsequent destruction) should also be seen as an indicator of the power of the coffee industry in many Latin American countries, especially Brazil, which has long been one of the region's biggest producers. This is because coffee producers were able to marshal the power of the state to provide price support for their product at a time when every part of the economy was suffering. This elasticity of supply also created a tendency for coffee elites to join together as a powerful interest group that could exert pressure on the state to engage in price support for the coffee industry (Knight 2014, 2018). Coffee is unique in that it continues to grow year after year unless the entire coffee plant is removed from the ground, which means that regardless of the price of coffee on the international market, coffee will continue to be produced. These sorts of government price supports were common in Latin America during the Great Depression due to the urgency of the economic crisis and the power of the coffee elite.

In addition, since coffee is sold on an international market, any domestic price support will also have an effect on the price of coffee coming from other states. Due to the sheer size of the Brazilian coffee industry, it could have an outsized impact on the market and would be especially helpful in providing price support to other coffee-growing countries. Given the dominance of Brazilian coffee on the international market, other coffee-producing countries saw a minor lift in prices from the actions of the Brazilian government. In places like El Salvador and Guatemala, however, most of the burden of the downturn in coffee was shifted to the workers, who saw lower coffee yields and prices cut deeply into their livelihoods (Paige 1997, 107). This, in turn, created a lot of labor friction between the underpaid workers who were unhappy with their bosses and the bosses who needed the workers to harvest the coffee so they could pay their debts. This conflict would set the stage for many of the rebel movements and violent civil wars that would plague countries like El Salvador, Guatemala, and Nicaragua from the 1930s to the 1980s.

The dislocation of the Great Depression also forced many small coffee farmers off their land and into other sectors if they were lucky and into unemployment and destitution if they were not. Similarly to many other parts of the world, throughout Latin America, the Great Depression helped to create a series of political movements among the working class that sought to reorder politics and society. This was especially true in Central America and saw the rise of revolutionary leaders such as Farabundo Martí in El Salvador, who would launch an uprising against the Salvadoran government in 1932 based in large part on the discontent of the coffee workers. "The poor prices on the world market for coffee had led to a decline in the number of harvester jobs available from November to February, and when there was work, the pay was very poor. Naturally, (Marti) took advantage of the discontent this caused" (Anderson 1992, 100). The uprising, known in El Salvador as La Matanza, is still one of the pivotal events in Salvadoran history. Although estimates vary, most scholars put the number killed at around 30,000, made up mostly of indigenous Salvadorans, many of whom were noncombatants.

The *matanza* is not only the definitive event between coffee laborers and the Salvadoran government of the twentieth century; it is one of the most important events in the history of Central America. The lessons learned by other political and military leaders would cause upheaval in the region that would culminate in the various civil wars in Central America in the 1980s. The Salvadoran example showed leaders in places like Nicaragua and Guatemala that violence was an effective tool against recalcitrant labor, and many leaders across Latin America would put this lesson into practice for several decades after the Great Depression.

The political reaction to the Great Depression also set in motion a tacit alliance between the traditional elites and the new military regimes that began to spring up around Latin America starting in the 1930s. As Knight (2014) observes, the old oligarchies, particularly in Central America, lost ground to the new personalist authoritarian strongman because of the Great Depression (292). This marriage of convenience between the old oligarchs, who got to continue running the economy, and the new military dictatorships, who got to run the government, persisted from the 1930s all the way to the 1980s in many parts of Latin America. El Salvador, again, provides the best example of this as one military dictator after another served as president from the 1930s to the start of the civil war in 1979. In Costa Rica, however,

> [T]he army played a secondary and limited role in maintaining the country's social order. After independence (1821), a process began to consolidate a centralized, non-militarized state. This process was facilitated because Costa Rica escaped the conflicts faced by liberals and conservatives, although not completely. The low level of conflict involved in the Ochomogo War of 1823

> and the War of the League in 1835 allowed a much faster modernization of the productive apparatus inherited from the colony and a link with the International Market. The basic institutions of conservative power such as the Church, colonial authorities and the traditional elite as large landowners were weak. This was owing to Costa Rica's remoteness from centers of power, lack of precious metals and an important first nation component Faced with this weakness, they were unable to oppose the liberal project, or share views on the need for modernization that sought Costa Rica's "order and progress." (Vogt 2019, 19)

Once again, the politics and history of Costa Rica would set the country on a path that was significantly different from its neighbors as well as most of the other countries of Latin America. As the Great Depression would devastate Latin America, the Costa Rican military would only be a mild tool in elite attempts to control the population. By the end of the 1940s, the military in Costa Rica would cease to exist altogether.

THE GREAT DEPRESSION, MANUEL MORA, AND COSTA RICAN COMMUNISM

Not surprisingly, the Great Depression of the 1930s also hit the Costa Rican coffee industry particularly hard as demand for agricultural goods waned. In Costa Rica, like much of the rest of the world, the Great Depression encouraged many people to think about alternatives to capitalism as reliance on agricultural exports made the economic downturn especially acute. Throughout Central America, the 1930s were a time of social, political, and economic dislocation that encouraged the formation of leftist movements to confront the landed elite. The Great Depression ultimately put an end to direct rule by the coffee oligarchies and generated powerful oppositional movements that nearly brought down the social and economic structures created by the coffee elite (Paige 1997, 22).

These powerful oppositional movements saw the rise of Augusto Sandino in Nicaragua and Farabundo Marti in El Salvador, both of whom had a radical view of how the political system in their countries, as well as in the broader region, should be changed. This radicalism often pushed average citizens into the crosshairs of political violence at the hands of the government, which was greatly influenced by each country's coffee elite. The radicalism in countries such as Nicaragua and El Salvador often led to violent clashes between coffee workers and the government, whose power was enhanced by the use of the national military. The Communist Party of El Salvador used the dislocation of the Great Depression to push for a transformation of society.

Faced with a historic opportunity provided by a militant rural proletariat pushed to desperation by the depths of the Great Depression, and opposed by a unified and intransigent group of employers in the coffee industry, the Communist Party of El Salvador dogmatically rejected coalition with the "social fascists" of the democratic trade unions, or anyone else for that matter, and launched an insurrection entirely on its own. The party's defeat, and the subsequent massacre of most of its followers, was the defining event in modern Salvadoran political history. It extinguished the left, indeed almost any cultural memory of the left, for another 50 years. (Paige 1999, 788)

The communist leader in Costa Rica during the 1930s was the altogether different Manuel Mora Valverde. Mora, who once famously said, "if it were necessary to destroy liberty and all of those attributes of the human personality in order to realize Marxist doctrine then he would be the principal adversary of socialism," (Paige 1997, 137), was not the sort of radical seen in El Salvador and Nicaragua. Rather than organizing the masses in a manner that led to terrible violence, Mora and the communists became the primary vehicle of the Costa Rican labor movement, which would have more similarities to a European-style social democracy than to the communist movements of its neighbors. This labor activism was especially evident in the fight between banana workers and the United Fruit Company in the 1930s, which made Mora a central figure in the labor movement from that moment forward.

The fight between banana workers and the United Fruit Company culminated in the Great Banana Strike of 1934 in Limón on the Atlantic coast. This situation was particularly complex as it concerned traditional labor issues, exacerbated by the effects of the Great Depression and issues of race, as many of the workers had been brought in from the Caribbean to work the banana fields of Costa Rica. As with other agricultural enterprises, the Great Depression deeply affected the export of bananas, and the industry went into a major slump. In this context, the Costa Rican government declared that there would be no more work visas for foreign nationals (Koch 1977, 348), an aggressive move toward excluding blacks from the labor market that had been percolating in Costa Rica throughout the Great Depression. This created a lot of crosscutting tensions that combined concerns over labor with racial animus.

A six-week banana plantation strike began in October. The strike was organized by whites and since blacks generally did not participate, it strained relations between the races. On the Old Line, workers (mostly whites) armed with machetes prevented small farmers (mostly blacks) from delivering fruit, but work continued as usual in the Estrella division where three-quarters of

> plantation workers were black peasants recruited locally. The docks, manned by two-thirds blacks, operated throughout the strike. Strike leader Manuel Mora made headlines in the English-language press by referring to "the damned blacks" [los malditos negros], and old timers recall that whites called them zopilotes ["black crows" or, literally, "turkey buzzards"]. (Koch 1977, 348)

Although there was certainly an ugly element to the Costa Rican strike, the difference between the outcomes of the 1932 Matanza in El Salvador and the Great Banana Strike of 1934 is that in Costa Rica the strike was not met with widespread violence against the strikers from the government at the behest of the coffee elite. In addition, the 1934 strike in Costa Rica was able to improve the lives of banana workers as the settlement of the strike mandated an 8-hour day and wage increases. It also codified the preference for Costa Rican workers over black Caribbean workers who had migrated to Costa Rica, a measure that would limit the citizenship rights of black Costa Ricans until the end of the Costa Rican civil war (Koch 1977, 349). The 1934 strike was also the impetus for a lot of the labor organization that has occurred in Costa Rica since that time. "In Costa Rica, organized banana workers staged in 1934 the most famous strike of the republic's history, provided crucial support for the populist governments of the 1940s, fought as militias in the 1948 civil war, presented regimes after 1948 with their main labor problem, and remained the most powerful sup- porters of the Left through the early 1980s" (Marquardt 2002, 5).

Similarly to other political groups that came to the forefront during the 1930s, the Costa Rican communist movement was initially focused on revolutionary change. The 1934 strike was not without violence and the threat of violence from the party as well as against them, but under Mora's leadership, the party quickly became more reform-minded. This perspective is deeply rooted in the pacific tradition of Costa Rica and the fact that, unlike its neighbors, Costa Rican elites were much more reform-minded than those elsewhere. Mora's personal biography also incorporated aspects of early radicalism tempered by a strong desire to work within the system toward reform. His father was a cabinet maker, and the family suffered greatly when he was exiled for opposing the Tinoco regime after the coup d'etat. From there, his student experience included associations with radical communist professors and fellow students but also with elites interested in reforming the system, including future president Rafael Angel Calderón (Paige 1997, 139–140).

The Communist Party of Costa Rica was founded on June 16, 1931, by a small group of intellectuals to compete in the 1932 special municipal elections in San José. Soon thereafter, the Costa Rican Congress declared it illegal, and the name was changed to Bloque de Obreros y Campesinos (Bloc of Workers and Peasants). They won two seats on the council (Seligson 1980, 70). The comparison between this action—declaring the Communist Party illegal but accepting a name change and allowing them to run candidates in the election—is a good illustration of the political differences between Costa Rica and its neighbors, where communist activity was usually a prelude to violence.

That being said, the popularity of the Communist Party, coupled with its labor activism in the agricultural sector, made the traditional coffee elites very nervous. While the Communist Party was never a serious electoral contender, it did become an important voice, and Mora's leadership and organization made it an important political movement during his lifetime, with the height of his power and influence occurring from the mid-1930s to the late 1940s. While Mora and the communists did not have a large enough role in elected government to enact changes, their advocacy and ultimately Mora's desire for reform rather than revolution, particularly with regard to socioeconomic change, forced other political parties to adopt what would become Costa Rica's social democratic model.

In this context, León Cortés Castro, a candidate in the 1936 presidential election, became the main opponent of communism in Costa Rica and promised to confront them at every opportunity. The Great Depression created an internal debate in many countries between the relative merits of communism and fascism, and Costa Rica was no different. Cortés "was influenced by fascist ideas and was supported by the quite substantial German community in Costa Rica" (Høivik and Aas 1981, 335). As such, Cortés became the main vehicle of anti-communism and pressed communism as a major issue in his campaign for the presidency. Although the economic upheaval helped the communists to organize workers in events like the banana strike, the chaotic nature of those strikes and the upheaval they caused meant that the Costa Rican government had little trouble characterizing the strike leaders (Mora among them) as agitators. Yet, Mora was still allowed to run for president despite the anti-communist rhetoric from Cortés and others. The campaign was successful as Cortés won the 1936 presidential election in a landslide with 60.2 percent of the vote to 34.5 percent for his opponent Octavio Béeche Argüello, while Manuel Mora Valverde, despite his success in building his movement, received 5.3 percent (Nohlen 2005, 167). When a candidate from the Bloc of Workers and Peasants won an election, the Cortés government found a way to disqualify them from serving. For instance, when the party won a seat in Congress, Cortés dissolved the Electoral Tribunal and did not allow the election winner to be seated (Hiltunen Biesanz et al. 1999, 28–29).

The combination of a burgeoning desire to transform into a legitimate long-term democracy, the labor unrest of the Great Depression, and the desire among factions not associated with the coffee elite, particularly those engaged in other agricultural sectors, to diminish the power of the coffee elite, ushered in a number of measures that would serve to weaken the coffee elite in the decade or so prior to the civil war. The first major step was the creation of the Asociación Nacional de Productores de Café (the forerunner of ICAFE) in 1930 to monitor the relationships between different-sized producers and exporters.

Unlike many other coffee-growing countries, the majority of Costa Rican coffee is grown by small farmers and then sold to a *beneficio,* who then processes the coffee. *Beneficios* are the key element in the Costa Rican coffee industry because they accept coffee from the fields and process it into an exportable good. Many farmers, especially smallholders, do not have the equipment they need to process coffee and must therefore sell it to a *beneficio* in order to have it processed. Part of the reason this is necessary is due to the complexity of processing coffee, which, after arriving from the farm usually via pickup truck, must be washed, pulped (a process in which the coffee seed is expelled from the outer fruit portion of the coffee cherry), and then dried. In Costa Rica, many farmers use large concrete pads to dry the coffee naturally in the sun. This not only costs nothing more than the labor to place it there and turn it so it dries evenly, but sun drying is usually considered a superior method that creates a higher-quality final product. Sometimes coffee is dried in large industrial dryers if the farmer does not have the room to dry it in the sun (or does not want to take the time needed), or the harvest is so bountiful that there is not enough room to dry it all on the pads. This is usually necessary to ensure that the coffee does not spoil due to being wet.

The Asociación Nacional de Productores de Café was created in response to the growth of the *recibidor* system, which had become much more efficient in collecting coffee from farmers since the advent of motorized vehicles (Seligson 1980, 35–36) due to the difficulties in using ox carts (the traditional method of transporting coffee in Costa Rica) to take coffee to market. The *recibidor* system, still in use in Costa Rica today, consists of small facilities placed around the countryside that allow farmers to drop off harvested and unprocessed coffee at a *beneficio* without needing to drive all the way to the main facility. While convenient for farmers, under this system, "the larger better-financed *beneficios* were able to out-compete the smaller ones in their immediate areas and could thereby drive them out of business." (Seligson 1980, 34)

The effect of the growth of the *recibidor* system pushed out many of the small and medium-sized *beneficios* as the largest ones could pay more for the farmers' coffee. In addition, "there was increasing suspicion on the part of the producers and govern- ment alike that the owners of the coffee (*beneficios*) and export houses were failing to pay a fair price to the producers and the appropriate amount of taxes to the government" (Seligson 1977, 222). In reaction to this, in 1933, the Costa Rican government created the Junta de Liquidaciones de Café "to set the price that each *beneficio* was to pay the producer; it based its calculations on the quality of the coffee and set a maximum profit of the *beneficio* at 12 percent. This sort of regulation was unheard of in Costa Rica, and the government had never intervened in the coffee industry in a manner such as this and the coffee elite, of course, did all they could to make certain they had a majority vote on the Junta de Liquidaciones de Café" (Seligson 1980, 36–37).

In this way, the politics and economics of the 1930s created the template for the upheaval of the 1940s in Costa Rica, as an increasing amount of pressure was applied to Costa Rican society generally and coffee farmers in particular. The two main forces encompassed those who pushed for more socioeconomic rights and the traditional coffee elites who (mostly) pushed against it. In addition, the development of the banana industry, mostly on the Atlantic Coast, meant that coffee was not as vital to the Costa Rican economy as it had been. This created a complex mix of politics, which continued to weaken the coffee elite and rendered them politically homeless. While the civil war of 1948 was the knockout blow for the power of the coffee elite, it would never be the same after the reforms of the 1930s, and its downward power trajectory would never reverse.

Another important social transformation that came to the forefront in the late nineteenth century and then accelerated in the time before the civil war were the demands of Costa Rica's burgeoning middle class. Not only did the nature of Costa Rica's historical development help to create a middle class with all of the usual preferences for the accouterments of middle-class life, it also imbued them with a pacific nature and a democratic self-identity. These translated into a desire to transform Costa Rican society, but more importantly, to modernize it. Costa Ricans have long been proud of their political and social systems, especially as they relate to the same systems in neighboring countries. The generations of Costa Ricans between 1889 and 1948 strongly desired to construct a democratic Costa Rica free from the strongman politics of the region and the chaos that too often affected the other states in Central America. These desires put a lot of pressure on the political system for reform.

As the Great Depression gave way to World War II and then the Cold War, many politicians in the United States saw the labor uprisings and the supposed leftist politics of the region as proof that communist agitators had infiltrated many Latin American governments. However, as Paige (1997, 3) summarizes, "North American policy makers saw the Central American conflicts as episodes in the cold war, they were in fact deeply rooted in the social and economic structures of the region. These structures in turn were shaped by a single commodity that has dominated these small export economies from the nineteenth century to the present—coffee." Authoritarian leaders in places like Managua and Guatemala City knew that casting any labor strife as communism could put them in line for large amounts of money from the United States to fight communism.

IMPORT SUBSTITUTION INDUSTRIALIZATION AND THE END OF THE INTERNATIONAL COFFEE AGREEMENT

The end of the Great Depression also caused a lot of self-reflection around the world regarding the manner in which the world economy functions, and Latin America was no different. The major impetus for change came from Argentine Economist Raul Prebisch in a paper entitled, "The Economic Development of Latin America and its Principal Problems," presented in Havana, Cuba, in 1949. challenged the prevailing assumptions about international trade from a structuralist perspective and the place of Latin America in the world economy as an exporter of primary goods and an importer of finished goods. Presented at the Havana Conference of 1949, Prebisch "questioned the international division of labor and urged more active participation of the State in the industrialization process to in this way do away with dependency and generate an anti-cyclical policy that entailed the displacement of productive factors, not always easy to make reality" (Fresneda 2016, 123).

Usually known as the "Prebisch-Singer" thesis, the ideas of unequal terms of trade and the need to boost intra-regional trade served as the basis for dependency theory as well as the economic ideas of import substitution industrialization (ISI). Dependency theory is a broader set of ideas that argue Latin America, as a region peripheral to the world's biggest economies, has suffered from this relationship and is best served by cutting ties with the developed world. It further argues that the unequal power relationship between the developed and developing world means that poor countries are exploited and underdeveloped as a result of their relationships with larger economies rather than having a more neutral relationship with them. The strongest manifestation of this has been through policies oriented toward import substitution industrialization, which was utilized by a number of Latin American governments into the 1970s and in some forms persists to this day.

ISI policies argue that the best way to industrialize is to limit imports from abroad so that an economy can produce those items domestically and thus boost its own economy. In many parts of Latin America, these policies provided a short-term boost to economic growth; however, the drawbacks to such an economic plan became apparent by the mid-1960s. As Irwin (2020,

20) argues, "the decline of import substitution as a policy idea accelerated after empirical studies from the mid-1960s began identifying the impact and cost of import restrictions." In addition, ISI strategies tend to fail over time because the market for domestic goods in a developing economy is too small for large-scale production, which means, among other things, that there is too little employment. A small amount of domestic production also is unable to satisfy the needs of society when imports are limited by the state. Despite ISI's decline in popularity, the ideas that promulgate ISI remain and are often popular among nationalist and populist politicians who seek to limit exposure to the world economy and protect their home markets.

At about the same time ISI was falling out of fashion, the world's largest coffee consumers and producers came together to sign the International Coffee Agreement (ICA) in 1962. The purpose of the agreement was to regulate the coffee market in an attempt to stabilize prices and production to benefit coffee farmers in the long-term. The ICA has been renewed and extended in various forms since its inception, and these renewals and extensions have often been controversial. States have left the ICA as different facets of the negotiations have broken down, sometimes joining and dropping out of the agreement at various junctures only to rejoin later. Most prominently, the United States left the ICA in 1989, rejoined in 2005, only to exit again in 2018, and has yet to rejoin (Daily Coffee News 2018). In the original treaty, the ICA used import and export quotas to boost the price of coffee for producers, and its collapse meant that the price of coffee on the international market fell precipitously, particularly as the international supply of coffee boomed. "The collapse of the ICA in 1989 and removal of quotas as part of a global deregulation of international markets resulted in market saturation of Robusta coffee from Vietnam and Brazil and significant fluctuations in global prices" (Vogt 2019, 49).

The ICA collapsed due to the following reasons: first, it was difficult to coordinate supply and demand under the quota system because of the unpredictability of growing any agricultural product, as supply can vary widely year by year. Since many large coffee-producing countries found themselves with a large amount of oversupply, they found it necessary to sell their excess coffee to nonmember countries at a reduced price. Not surprisingly, this was not popular among large importer countries in the agreement, which partially explains the unstable membership in the agreement. This unstable membership is another reason the ICA collapsed. The withdrawal of the United States was one of the final blows to the agreement due to the large amount of coffee it imported each year.While the ICA continues to operate under new agreements, without the quota system implemented in the initial agreement, it has very little effect on the coffee market. The collapse of the ICA has once again made the price of coffee fluctuate significantly on the international market.

However, the quota system was a difficult method to achieve price stability because one of the most noteworthy facets of the international coffee market is the wide price fluctuations that create high peaks and low valleys in price. Given that coffee production is beholden to multiple unpredictable factors of production, including the weather, problems arising from pests and diseases, and the general difficulty of farming, there is a tendency for coffee to be more volatile than other commodities.In addition, the coffee production cycle is different. A lot of coffee around the world is collected by small farmers without a contract. When the price goes up, these small producers collect their coffee and sell it, which increases supply. As the supply of coffee increases, the price goes down, and fewer small producers think it is worth the work to collect it, so they stop selling it. The supply then goes down again, the price goes up, and the small producers again collect and sell their coffee, and the cycle continues.

The oversupply of coffee not only contributed to the end of the ICA but also to the coffee crisis of the late 1990s. “The relative supply scarcity of the mid 1990s, caused largely by climatic conditions, was followed by a short period of moderately high prices that compensated for the losses incurred by the dismantling in 1989 of the International Coffee Agreement’s quota system. However this situation prompted a surge in production that substantially altered the global supply structure and was the cause of the worst coffee crisis ever seen in terms of growers’ incomes” (Osorio 2004, 1). The global oversupply of coffee was due to the improvement of farming techniques over the years, allowing coffee farmers to produce ever-larger quantities of coffee. Many countries that were traditionally engaged in coffee production, such as Brazil, as well as new coffee-producing countries such as Vietnam, began producing huge quantities of coffee that flooded the market and lowered prices precipitously. Brazil has long been one of the largest producers of coffee in the world and produces coffee at a very wide range of quality levels. Countries such as Vietnam, however, entered the coffee market in a very different way.

Vietnam is an interesting example and is now the second-largest producer of coffee in the world, behind only Brazil. Although coffee was first cultivated in Vietnam during the mid-nineteenth century, the modern Vietnamese coffee industry dates to 1986 when the government transitioned from a planned to a free-market economy and the production of coffee exploded. Unlike most countries in Latin America, which produce Arabica beans, the Vietnamese coffee industry produces Robusta beans, which are usually considered lower-quality because they are generally more bitter with a higher caffeine content. Robusta coffee is also easier to grow than Arabica and produces a much higher yield. In addition, Robusta is easier to manage, grows at a lower altitude, and is more resistant to disease. Robusta coffee gro in places like Vietnam, therefore, tends to be used for instant coffee or is blended into higher-quality coffee to save money and is often used in many inexpensive grocery store brands in the United States and Europe.

The overproduction of Robusta, in particular, not only negatively affects the price of coffee generally but will also have an effect on the price of Arabica as well. As such, products like Vietnamese Robusta will lessen demand for Arabica as it is used to make a less expensive and lower-quality final product. While many coffee-producing countries have focused on high-quality coffee, Costa Rica, for instance, actually outlawed the production of Robusta in 1988 (repealed in 2018) to focus on the production of higher-quality coffee. Other countries have pursued Robusta as a crop that is easier to cultivate and manage. The growth and scale of Robusta coffee production in Vietnam are staggering. "When the Vietnam war ended in 1975 the country was on its knees, and economic policies copied from the Soviet Union did nothing to help. Collectivising agriculture proved to be a disaster, so in 1986 the Communist Party carried out a U-turn—placing a big bet, at the same time, on coffee. Coffee production then grew by 20–30 percent every year in the 1990s" (Summers 2014).

WORLD WAR II AND THE COSTA RICAN CIVIL WAR

As the middle class pushed for reform, Costa Ricans voted for presidents who were generally in favor of improvement to the democratic process and to cultural and economic growth, and were pro-education. The fact that most elites, regardless of party affiliation, were dedicated to some level of reform helps to explain why communism gave way to social democracy after the civil war. In addition, the global fight against fascism and the inclusion of the communist Soviet Union in the allied cause helped to give a veneer of legitimacy to many of the ideas of the communists, although not necessarily to communism itself. Many of these ideas became even more attractive as the problems from the Great Depression were extended by the onset of World War II. The problem for the coffee industry was that a lack of demand gave way to markets that were virtually closed to Costa Rican coffee due to trade restrictions placed by the United States in response to the war. For instance, in 1940, Costa Rica exported 8,568,377 kilograms of coffee to England; however, with U.S. imposed restrictions placed on exports, there were multiple years (1941, 1944, 1945) in which no coffee was sold to England whatsoever. In November of 1940, in an attempt to alleviate the problems of a lack of market for their coffee and to make sure that Latin America did not suffer a severe economic depression due to restricted trade and to guarantee their loyalty in World War II, the United States agreed to buy the bulk of Latin

America's coffee. To simplify the process, the United States purchased coffee at a single price regardless of quality (Seligson 1980, 35). Since quality, rather than large-scale production, had long been the hallmark of Costa Rican coffee, a buyer with no concern for quality greatly changed the calculus of the *beneficios* and their relationship with producers, and served to exacerbate problems between small and large producers, and many smaller producers lost their operations during this time.

> Domestic relations between coffee growers and processing firms, which had become tense, were moderated by legislation and public institutions, notably the Coffee Institute. Farmers took less care of their groves and did not plant new ones, cut their labor costs by harvesting ripe and unripe berries simultaneously, and kept waiting for prices to improve. Processing firms cut their own costs by paying lower prices for the harvested fruit, by mixing coffee from different altitudes, and by giving less labor-intensive attention to quality, which undoubtedly suffered. The number of processing plants dropped by one-third, while the banks took over and operated foreclosed facilities. Each remaining beneficio received coffee from a larger number of farmers at greater distances. Some exporters mixed coffee from higher and lower altitudes, and overall quality suffered. The number of export firms dropped once again during this period, and at the end of World War II the four largest ones controlled four-fifths of the volume exported. (Samper 2010, 74)

The economic, social, and political upheaval created by the Great Depression, coupled with the labor strife of that period, served to magnify the difficulties of World War II, and Costa Rica reached a boiling point. In addition to issues over price and the relations between different sectors of the domestic coffee industry, the relationship between the coffee elite and the government was further exacerbated by the election in 1940 of Rafael Angel Calderón Guardia. A cancer doctor who had long been supported by the coffee elite, Calderón quickly turned his back on them and pursued a social democratic platform. According to Rosenberg (1981), few members of the coffee elite openly disagreed with the need for a social security system, but on the heels of the Great Depression and World War II, many thought that it was not the right time to increase taxes, especially with Calderón's poor managerial skills (290). It was also widely believed by Costa Ricans that Calderón mismanaged the early stages of World War II when Costa Rica, like many of its neighbors, was still suffering from the aftershocks of the Great Depression, and war-related shortages and lack of access to many European markets and low coffee prices hit especially hard.

Calderón's social agenda "led to a break with the traditional elite, and in 1943 Calderón entered into an alliance with the Catholic Church and the Communist Party (renamed Vanguardia Popular to facilitate Church support)" (Olander 1996, 467). The alliance between their traditional ally Calderón and Mora and his communists was a crushing blow to many coffee farmers, especially the larger operations. After his election, Calderón proposed a number of left-leaning policy proposals that did not worry many Costa Ricans in and of themselves, but many people were concerned with Calderón's administrative and managerial abilities which affected his ability to efficiently put such policies into action.

> His inaugural address outlined measures by which his government proposed to foment the social, cultural and economic development of the nation. He promised particular attention to the less well developed areas of Costa Rica, such as Guanaecaste and the Atlantic region which had largely been abandoned by the United Fruit Company. He pledged himself to a revision of the entire system of taxation on the just basis of capacity to contribute. He promised to give a new impulse to rural credit, to provide for a program of land distribution through the National Bank, and to initiate a program of low-cost housing. He proposed to found a national university that would orient public opinion on social questions and promote the general progress of the republic. As a contribution to the welfare of all, he promised to institute a system of social security. (Bell 1971, 27)

Although Calderón proffered these reforms, the ideology as well as the power base behind them were not particularly well conceived and he was never specific with his intentions during his presidential campaign.

> Calderón's programs were not methodically conceived. His social-security program, introduced in 1941, was not presented in a larger reformist package, nor was it the result of an articulate or well-defined working-class or other interest-group pressure. It was an elitist reform, paternalistically sponsored by the state. Coupled with Calderon's poor political and administrative management of the Costa Rican state and his close association with the Catholic Church, this reform cost him heavily in conservative circles, a situation that Calderon did not realize until mid- 1942. It was then that he consciously sought an alternative following. State-sponsored social reform through "social guarantees" and the "labor code" was used explicitly to generate that support. (Rosenberg 1981, 280)

While Costa Rica had brief interludes of authoritarianism, the country had long been able to stay on the path of democratization. This path was deeply threatened when, in 1944, constitutionally unable to run for a consecutive term as president, Calderón supported the candidacy of Teodoro Picado Michalski, widely seen as Calderón's puppet. In fact, the 1944 election of Picado provided election integrity as yet another point of contention in Costa Rican politics, as those opposed to Picado (and by extension Calderón) called the 1944 Costa Rican presidential election the most fraudulent in the country's history (Olander 1996, 468). The selection of Picado as his successor and the fraudulent nature of the election meant that Calderón had become the domineering authoritarian that many segments of Costa Rican society had begun to fear during his presidency.

The upheaval in Costa Rican politics that had intensified during the Great Depression and now included problems with election integrity set Costa Rica on the path toward irreconcilable differences. After the questionable election of Picado, Costa Ricans took to the streets as they had during the Tinoco administration a generation before, in an attempt to show their displeasure. Picado, sensing trouble, used the military to quell unrest, which did little to allay the fears of the populace over the increasing authoritarianism of the regime. These fears came true when the disputed election of 1948, which was won by Otilio Ulate, was annulled by the legislature at the request of Calderón under the guise of "fraud." This move deeply angered many Costa Ricans, and electoral integrity was pushed even further to the front of their minds as fraud was used both to secure a victory (Picado in 1944) and to try and prevent another candidate from defeating the Picado-Calderón faction in 1948. These episodes also turned Costa Rica, for a short time, into a sort of Cold War "hot spot" as popular opinion turned against the communists, who were a part of Calderón's coalition. While Mora was considerably less militant than many other communist leaders of the 1930s, particularly in Central America, his ideology and ties to the Soviet Union also started to draw the attention of the United States. For instance, writing just after the civil war, Joseph F. Thorning (1949, 49–50) in *World Affairs* refers to Mora as the "Soviet Chieftain in Costa Rica" and states that Calderón decided to annul the election under pressure from Soviet agents.

The seminal event in Costa Rican history, the 1948 civil war, which reshaped Costa Rican politics in myriad ways, began on March 12, 1948, just 11 days after the annulment of the 1948 presidential election. It also represented a very rare event in the country's history—Costa Rican politicians, unable to solve their problems through negotiation, tried to do so on the battlefield. Lehoucq (1991) calls the Costa Rican civil war "the most significant breakdown of emerging democratic practices in what many believe is a country with a democratic destiny" (37). The civil war lasted 6 weeks and resulted in over 2000 deaths (Hiltunen Biesanz et al. 1999, 31) and would end when government forces surrendered to the rebels under José Figueres Ferrer after they took Cartago and before they could move on to the capital, San José.

Figueres, known in Costa Rica as Don Pepe, was a successful coffee farmer and rope maker who was exiled by Calderón in 1942 for his anti-regime politics. According to national myth, Figueres put together a ragtag group of young idealists upset with the Calderón-Picado faction and desirous of making Costa Rica a free and fair democracy that takes care of its citizens. While this might have been true at some level, Figueres, while exiled for his opposition to the Calderón government, spent a lot of his time planning a way to return to politics and topple the regime. He was given the opportunity to return as an anti-Calderón hero and start the revolution he had long sought when the 1948 presidential election was annulled. He also put together a force known as the Caribbean Legion, whose goal was to topple the government in Costa Rica and then to do likewise in other countries that found themselves under the yoke of an authoritarian regime.

During the civil war, Figueres headquartered his forces in the small coffee farming town of Santa Maria de Dota, in the Los Santos coffee region of central Costa Rica. A visitor to the town would be hard-pressed to see any evidence of the revolutionary hero's time there, except for a few monuments around town and a local or two happy to discuss the monuments in the park and the fact that his headquarters were in the local elementary school. The most important of these monuments is a statue in the main square, which commemorates a young soldier who was tortured and subsequently killed when he would not give up the location of Don Pepe.

When Figueres was victorious in the civil war, he led a junta that governed Costa Rica at the conclusion of the conflict as a placeholder to get the country through the conflict. The junta governed for 18 months, but then turned the government over to Otilio Ulate, who finished the term that many Costa Ricans thought he won in the 1948 election. Given that this was a complex time in Costa Rican politics, paradoxes from this period abound. One of the main paradoxes is that since many of the social reforms put forth by Calderón were actually very popular with many Costa Ricans, President Ulate put forth a number of additional social reforms that went beyond even what Calderón had proposed. Not surprisingly, proffering social reforms beyond even what Calderón had suggested further alienated the coffee growers, who found themselves with no ideological home. Throughout the previous fifty years or so, for the most part, the coffee elite had supported the more conservative political parties in Costa Rica. This changed, however, with both Calderón's policies as well as his alliance with the communists (not to mention the electoral integrity issues!) and served to detach much of the coffee elite from their traditional political alliances. To their chagrin, the coffee elite would also realize that now in office, Ulate and later Figueres (elected in 1952) would extract much of the money for Costa Rica's social programs from the revenues generated by the coffee industry. The fact that the coffee elite were more or less politically homeless coupled with a government that sought to build Costa Rica with tax money taken from the coffee elite greatly diminished the power of the coffee farmers and affected their standing in the Costa Rican economy.

With all the upheaval in Costa Rica during the first half of the twentieth century, culminating in a short but intense civil war, the 1949 Constitution permanently changed the structure of the Costa Rican government and provided a legal finality to many of the issues Costa Ricans had argued and fought about for more than 50 years. The most prominent of which is contained in Title 1, Article 12—the permanent dissolution of the military (Constitución Politíca de la República de Costa Rica). It is important to note that the military in Costa Rica is not merely banned by the constitution, but is outlawed—in Spanish, "Se proscribe el Ejército como institución permanente." (The Army is outlawed as a permanent institution) (Constitución Politíca de la República de Costa Rica). This is an important distinction because it means that the military is not merely banned, as if on some sort of hiatus, but that it is outside of the law permanently in Costa Rica.

While the Costa Rican military was never particularly powerful, it was periodically used by presidents to put down protests or strikes and was often seen as the enforcement arm of coffee interests, though it was used in this way considerably less than in other states in Central America. The military also never played much of a role in Costa Rican history due to the small population and the fact that there were never many economic assets to protect or, frankly, many enemies to protect them from. After World War II, Costa Rica turned to the United States and signed a treaty that ensured the United States would intervene if Costa Rica were ever attacked, which exacerbated the military's weakness and lack of development. This contributed to the military being easily defeated by Figueres' forces during the civil war,

> The Costa Rican Army, however, continued to be a weak institution. It consisted of about 1,000 men, had one unit with light combat vehicles, and was equipped with North American weapons. The officers were drawn from supporters of each administration, were members of the local elite, and had little military background or training. On change of administration, the officers were formally promoted and then dismissed. (Høivik and Aas 1981, 335)

The combination of Figueres' defeat of the communist forces in the civil war, the burgeoning Cold War, and the need for support from Washington meant that Don Pepe quickly became an avid anti-communist. As Booth (1987, 49) points out, "anticommunism has been a key feature of Costa Rican political culture since the late 1940s, in part because of resentment of certain abuses of power and the 1948 electoral fraud during the Communist party's participation in power from 1942 to 1948." Due to these realities the Costa Rican civil war also ended the influence of the Communist Party as it was outlawed in the 1949 constitution (the prohibition was repealed in 1975) (Constitución Politíca de la República de Costa Rica Artículo 98). Despite the ignominious end, the social democratic policies, labor, and social security laws supported by Mora and others remain in force to this day. In addition, the fact that communism was regulated and banned, then reinstated, yet contributed ideas that became law, is one of the chief illustrations of how Costa Rican politics, especially during the time between the Great Depression and the end of the Cold War, were considerably different from the regional norm.

Part of the reason that Figueres was able to cultivate a pro-American and anti-communist image is that he had long been associated with the United States, was an admirer of many aspects of its political and social systems, and maintained close ties with many politicians in Washington.

> Figueres had traveled to the United States in the 1920s. Originally, he had planned to study at the Massachusetts Institute of Technology, but instead he spent most of his time in the Boston Public Library reading books on economics, history, and sociology. The writings of Thomas Jefferson, Leo Tolstoy, and Charles Fournier strongly influence his ideological development. When he returned to Costa Rica in the late 19 purchased a finca and worked tirelessly to create a thriving business. A strong admirer of the New Deal, Don Pepe also implemented various experiments that included providing health care, education, and other benefits to his workers. Figueres never forgot his American experience and visited the United States many times. He also retained close ties with Americans through his wives, both of whom were US citizens. (Longley 1994)

The 1949 constitution also put finality to other issues in Costa Rica and, as such, created a new political order starting in the second half of the twentieth century. The constitution incorporates a number of social issues into Costa Rican life that had long been under national discussion. For instance, the constitution gives foreigners the same individual and social rights as Costa Rican citizens, and it also ensures a number of social rights and guarantees including adequate distribution of wealth, the right to privacy, and a number of rights regarding unionization and workers' rights (Constitución Politíca de la República de Costa Rica, Título III). Another important element of the 1949 constitution is Artículo VII, which establishes the centrality of education in Costa Rican society. It not only makes public education free and compulsory, but also sets a minimum percentage of the national budget that must be set aside for education (8 percent) (Constitución Politíca de la República de Costa Rica). In this way, the constitution codified a Costa Rica that was vastly different from the country that existed during the nineteenth century when the coffee growers were at the height of their power.

The Costa Rican civil war also permanently established the political movement of Pepe Figueres, who founded the Partido Liberación Nacional (PLN) in 1951 and transformed it into an important political force. Interestingly, despite Figueres' anti-communist views as well as his defeat of the communists on the battlefield, the PLN is a member of the Socialist International. As the leader of the PLN, Figueres was able to create an "electoral alliance and an ideological mythology as both the essential and the only legitimate Costa Rican reformist force and tradition" (Gudmundson 2021, 16). Figueres parlayed his victory in the civil war and his popularity with many Costa Ricans into multiple presidencies of Costa Rica. He was interim president from 1948–1949 and served two more full terms, 1953–1958 and 1970–1974. Due to this, and despite the national mythology, the PLN mostly consolidated their power in the time after the civil war by simultaneously proffering interventionist reforms while serving as an anti-communist outpost in Central America. According to Gudmundson (2021, 17):

> Figueres represented an extraordinarily attractive and skillful figure in this process, not only for his impeccable English or his U.S.-born first wife. He was able to successfully navigate rough waters as Cold War polarization deepened. He knew how to use his unquestionable anticommunist credentials, even when his policies and in favor of state intervention in the economy infuriated Cold war conservatives and militants equally at home and in Washington.

The PLN continues to be one of the most important forces in Costa Rican politics and has had a great deal of electoral success since the end of the civil war. Part of the reason that Figueres' movement has continued to be successful is that he was able to defeat the Calderónistas in the civil war, then returned power to the rightfully elected Ulate rather than persist in power himself, a move that was very rare during this time in other Central American political systems. In addition, the PLN set the post-civil war standard on what happens when a political party loses an election, as they did in 1958. "The 1958 election, when Mario Echandi was elected president of an anti-PLN coalition, laid the foundation for peaceful alternations in power. A two-party system gradually emerged, with the PLN competing against what eventually became the more conservative PUSC" (Social Christian Unity Party) (Perelló and Navia 2021, 90).

In addition to the previous provisions of the 1949 Constitution already discussed, the most important section of the constitution that diminished the power of the coffee elite was the establishment of various agricultural cooperatives, including cooperatives for coffee in Title 5, Article 64. The cooperative movement greatly shifted the power of the coffee industry from large estates to small and medium-sized enterprises. The cooperative system affected Costa Rican coffee farmers in two main ways. First, it created a regulatory framework for the manner in which farmers and *beneficios* interact, particularly with regard to the amount paid by the beneficio to the farmer when they deliver their coffee. Secondly, the cooperative system allows small farmers, through a public beneficio, to work together and provide a unified voice when they sell their coffee to the export market. For instance, an individual smallholder with a couple of hectares of coffee would not be able to sell that coffee to a large coffee company such as Starbucks or would have to do so via a farmgate sale—which literally means that the farmer sells coffee to the large company over the farmgate without any sort of permanent contract or relationship between the two. As part of a cooperative, a coffee farmer with a small operation can contribute coffee to the cooperative and have that coffee sold at a larger profit on the international market to a large multinational corporation. Cooperatives vary in size and structure; two prominent coffee cooperatives in Costa Rica located in the Los Santos region are CoopeTarrazú and CoopeDota, located in the cantons of Tarrazú and Dota, respectively. These cooperatives profoundly change the way that many small and medium coffee producers operate by giving them better access to the resources they need and, most especially to the international market.

In the beginning of the twentieth century, a burgeoning middle class put demands on the political system of Costa Rica to make changes to the political, economic, and social structures of the country. These ideas would see various ups and downs across that time period, but in the end, the civil war and its aftermath would permanently change the trajectory of Costa Rica and would also decrease the power of Costa Rican coffee growers. To many Costa Rican coffee farmers, it was also the beginning of the attitude among them that their lifestyle and livelihood were under attack. Since colonial times, they had enjoyed government and tax benefits and were at the center of Costa Rican culture. The debt crisis of the 1980s would serve to push coffee further to the periphery of the national economy as other revenue streams began to take precedence, most notably the emergence of ecotourism.

THE DEBT CRISIS OF THE 1980S

The next major problem facing the Costa Rican economy and its coffee industry was the debt crisis of the 1980s. The debt crisis in Latin America was caused by many factors, the most important of which was the inability of many states to continue making payments on their external debt, the first of which was Mexico in August of 1982. Mexico, like its neighbors, experienced a boom in commodities (especially oil) in the 1970s that led to massive borrowing from international lending institutions, with the subsequent bust making it impossible to meet their international debt obligations. "The major policy responses to the crisis have been stabilization programs and rescheduling of debt payments. The traditional stabilization programs centered around the contraction of aggregate demand, with tight monetary policies combined with attempts at reducing fiscal deficits." (Twomey 1989, 548)

The debt crisis of the 1980s represented the largest existential crisis to Costa Rica since the civil war and was a multifaceted crisis that affected every part of Costa Rica, according to Furlong (1987, 124).

> Costa Rica's economic, political and foreign difficulties cannot be overstated. The domestic difficulties, taken together, add to the worst series of problems the country has had to face since World War II and include: economic crises; budget deficits; bankruptcy of t country's largest state enterprise, the Costa Rican Development Corporation (CODESA); increased unemployment and lowered product lower commodity prices (for bananas, coffee, sugar, etc.); rural unrest, land invasions; strikes; and loss of jobs and income by the mid classes. Costa Ricans suffer greatly from an economic malaise which threatens not only the quality of life but also the entire democratic system.

The economic crisis in Costa Rica meant that between 1980 and 1982, the economy contracted by 9.4 percent and inflation was over 90 percent. This contributed to a 20 percent increase in those living below the poverty line, which sat at 54 percent of the population. In addition, Costa Rica suffered a severe terms of trade crisis as the price of imports soared while the price of exports plummeted. Ultimately, Costa Rica was forced to devalue its currency, which further exacerbated inflation (Hidalgo 2014). While there had been misgivings regarding the efficacy of import substitution industrialization, the economic problems that it created both in the region as well as in Costa Rica meant that decision-makers needed to formulate a new strategy for economic development.

Similarly to much of Latin America, the debt crisis of the 1980s was the final straw for import substitution industrialization (ISI) in Costa Rica. ISI is a system in which domestically produced goods are substituted for imported goods to lessen the reliance on foreign economies and was borne out of the experience of the Great Depression. Under an ISI strategy, rather than importing consumer goods, such as shoes, they are produced in the domestic market. Although ISI provides some positive growth initially, it is ultimately undone by a variety of factors. The trade barriers necessary for ISI mean that imported goods are often prohibitively expensive and thus provide a monopoly for domestic producers, who struggle to produce enough goods for the domestic market. This can lead to excessive overvaluation of the country's currency to provide price relief for needed consumer imports. In the Costa Rican example, as these issues started to ramp up, Costa Rica was buffeted with economic problems both internally and externally. As Hidalgo (2014, 127) writes:

> As foreign direct investment dried up, the current account deficit increased to 12.6 percent of GDP in 1980. Then-president Rodrigo Carazo (1978–1982) decided to resort to foreign financing to maintain the fixed exchange rate. Costa Rica's external debt quadrupled during his term in office. However, a rise in international interest rates aggravated the situation by increasing the cost of government financing. Instead of cutting public spending and getting rid of onerous state-owned enterprises, Carazo chose to deal with the government's deteriorating finances by printing money. Eventually the government was forced to devalue the currency. Inflation skyrocketed, sending hundreds of thousands of Costa Ricans into poverty.

Once the debt crisis of the 1980s started to improve, Costa Rica and the rest of the world's coffee producers were then hit with a major downturn in the coffee market due to the end of the International Coffee Agreement and the concurrent oversupply, both of which resulted in a sharp decrease in the price of coffee. The decrease in price, not surprisingly, led to a major upheaval in the Costa Rican coffee industry,

> The vast majority of the approximately 40,000 coffee farmers attempted to weather the 1989–1993 crisis by various means, hoping for better prices later on, but some could no longer care for their groves and shifted away from coffee production temporarily or altogether. Roughly 100 processing plants remained in operation, but ownership became more concentrated. Some private firms and cooperatives went bankrupt or sold plants and other assets to pay off debt, and four corporate groups processed close to one-third of the harvest. A few multinational corporations acquired major processing facilities and supply networks and became dominant in the export business. (Samper 2010, 75)

With the debt crisis and the end of the ISI system followed by the coffee crisis, Costa Rican decision-makers embarked on policies that opened their economy to foreign investment to increase the amount of capital coming into the country. They signed a number of free trade agreements and were able to attract large-scale foreign direct investment, most notably attracting a major facility to produce computer parts for the U.S.-based computer company Intel in the San José suburb of Alajuela. Attracting Intel to Costa Rica was a major milestone for the Costa Rican economy and indicated that Costa Rica was a prime location for foreign direct investment, particularly in the high-tech sector, and that agricultural exports, especially coffee, had further receded into the background as a developmental priority for the Costa Rican economy.

As a result, by the 1990s, Costa Rican policymakers had arrived at a completely new set of economic priorities for the country, one in which high-tech exports were now privileged, and agricultural products were on the backburner. Costa Rica wanted to diversify its economy from dependence on a small array of agricultural products, with coffee at its core, to a more diverse set of export offerings, a trend that had been in the works since at least the 1930s. In addition, the integration of the Costa Rican economy into the larger world system provided a prime opportunity for foreign direct investment. As such, Costa Rica's economic priorities by the early 1990s had become attracting foreign direct investment, particularly in the high-tech sector, the preservation of high-value agricultural products (especially coffee), and parlaying Costa Rica's vast ecological diversity into a new ecotourism industry.

The motivation for Costa Rican policymakers was not just to broaden economic activities as a bulwark against an economic downturn, but it is also important to understand the development of an ecotourism industry as a reaction to an environmental awakening in Costa Rica, due in large part to the country's rapid deforestation. "In the 1940s, 75% of Costa Rica was cloaked in lush rainforests. Then the loggers arrived, chainsaws in hand, and cleared the land to grow crops and raise livestock. While there is ongoing debate about the extent of reduction, it is thought that between a half and a third of forest cover had been destroyed by 1987" (CNN).

The coalescence of the debt crisis, the need to diversify Costa Rica's economy, concern over deforestation, and the inherent environmental ethic that came with it led directly to the development of an ecotourism industry. The development of a societal-wide environmental ethic that emerged in the 1980s and helped motivate the nascent ecotourism industry also had an impact on the coffee industry. Almost since the beginning of the coffee industry in the nineteenth century, coffee farms, and especially *beneficios*, were very often heavy polluters, and most coffee operations, especially large operations, are built next to a river so the coffee waste can be flushed downstream. Coffee processing creates a great deal of wastewater containing unwanted organic waste, including the pulp (the fruit of the plant), mucilage (the inner part of the fruit), and parchment (the outer covering of the coffee bean itself, removed for roasting). Coffee wastewater is, therefore, generally made of a high concentration of organic matter and suspended solids and is highly acidic (Ijanu et al. 2020).

Another part of Costa Rica's economic strategy resulting from the economic crisis is that, starting in the late 1980s, the Costa Rican government actually outlawed the production of lower-quality Robusta coffee beans so farmers were forced to exclusively grow Arabica varietals, which are widely considered to be of superior quality. Although the ban on Robusta beans ended in 2018, mostly due to the pressures of climate change on coffee farming since Robusta beans are considerably easier to grow, ICAFE had come under serious pressure to allow coffee farmers more flexibility in the crops they grow. That said, Costa Rican coffee farmers still overwhelmingly grow Arabica, particularly for the specialty market, as Robusta is usually a filler used to make instant coffee or in low-cost grocery store brands. Costa Rica has focused on the production of high-quality coffee rather than quantity because they do not have the amount of land needed to produce a large quantity of coffee, but they do have the sort of growing environment that leads to much higher-quality coffee.

COSTA RICA COFFEE IN HISTORICAL CONTEXT

In many important ways, the history of Costa Rica is the history of growing, processing, and exporting coffee, and the social and cultural importance of coffee cannot be overstated. It is also important to remember that Costa Rican historical development varies in significant ways from other coffee-growing countries in Latin America and especially from its neighbors in Central America. Coffee was the first major economic product in the country's history and it paid for much of the development for the first century and a half of Costa Rican history. However, the story of the Costa Rican coffee industry is one in which coffee has transitioned from the central economic enterprise of the country to one of considerably less importance. The power of the coffee elite was on the rise from independence until the time of the Great Depression, and since that time has been on a steady decline in its influence on Costa Rican politics, society, and economics. Since the early 1990s, Costa Rica has used a three-part economic plan as its major development strategy. First is high-tech manufacturing of things like computer parts and medical equipment. Second is the ecotourism industry, and the continued production of high-value agricultural products is a distant third. In fact, the two main agricultural exports in Costa Rica, coffee and bananas, both grow year after year and do not need to be planted and harvested each season, which ensures that coffee will continue to be important, at least to those in the coffee-growing regions of Costa Rica and to those who drink it.

Chapter 3

The Ecology of Coffee in Costa Rica

This chapter describes the ecological issues associated with creating and managing the plantation, harvesting coffee, and coffee processing. This *cradle-to-grave* approach is useful for identifying particularly ecologically harmful practices or, on the flip side, identifying practices that can have a particularly positive impact during the entire life cycle of coffee. The "cradle" in this analogy is the creation of the plantation, as well as the source of coffee plants. The "grave" for coffee is the destination of the waste products, including the spent cherries and coffee grounds. Between the cradle and the grave is the maintenance of the plantation (e.g., weed control) and plants (pruning and replacement). Because of the area that coffee impacts, as well as the intensity of those impacts, coffee farming is worthy of studying the ecological impacts. Of course, there are multiple ways to lessen the impacts of coffee farming, which this chapter includes. This chapter also examines the future of coffee and how emerging technologies will help increase coffee sustainability. Lastly, this chapter examines emerging threats to producing coffee sustainably in Costa Rica. The emerging threats include climate change, which is predictable in the sense that temperatures are going to increase and precipitation regimes change. But emerging threats also include the unpredictable. Increasing global trade has also resulted in an increase in the number of invasive species. What new species will be inadvertently imported to Costa Rica is unknown, and how these species will interact with native species (or other invasive species) cannot be predicted.

The preceding chapters discussed the importance of coffee in the politics, economics, and society of Latin America generally, and Costa Rica specifically. The ecological importance of coffee is the result of replacing tropical forests with a simpler ecosystem that is often maintained with inputs of herbicides, insecticides, and fertilizers. Moreover, coffee processing can use large amounts of water and produce large amounts of organic waste material. Together, the growing and processing of coffee have large impacts on biodiversity and ecosystem processes. A simple Google Scholar search in August 2024 for "coffee AND biodiversity loss" returned around 114,000 results!

Ecologically sustainable practices will be those that result in minimal loss of biodiversity, preserve soils for long-term use, and do not stress water systems (see Brundtland 1987 and, more specifically, https://sdgs.un.org/2030agenda). Another way to state ecological sustainability is to refer to the maintenance of ecosystem services, which are the natural processes that benefit humans (Costanza et al. 1997). Instances of ecosystem services abound in the coffee world: from bees (and other insects) pollinating coffee flowers to plants that hold the soil around coffee plants, to fungi breaking down leaves to make nutrients for coffee plants. Sustainable practices are those that maintain or at least do not diminish these important ecosystem services.

THE DEFORESTATION PROBLEM WITH COFFEE PLANTATIONS

Although coffee plants can be grown from seed directly in the field, most farmers have a nursery stock on site or purchase from a nursery. The nursery stock typically comes from seed, although cuttings can be used if the source plants have traits that are highly sought after, such as disease resistance. In nurseries, the small size of young coffee plants allows them to be packed together tightly, and these young plants are kept under a shade canopy since they are more sensitive to the intense tropical sun. In the nursery, young seedlings are grown in different types of containers, but thin plastic containers of about 1.5 liters are commonly used. These containers can easily be cut away just before planting. Plants stay in the nursery for six to eighteen months before being planted in the field. Not only does the nursery provide a chance for the seedlings to develop under the watchful eye of the farmer, but it also provides an opportunity for experimentation with various coffee varieties to see if they can thrive and produce a new coffee, oftentimes for the luxury market. When the young plants reach the desired height, they are ready to be planted on the plantation.

Many coffee plantations are located where the forest cover has already been removed and the farmers are simply replacing existing land use, such as cattle ranching or some other crop. One potential issue with converting cattle pasture into coffee plantations is soil compaction. After years of cattle moving over pastures, their weight compacts soils, making water infiltration more difficult (Centeri 2022). Before and during the expansion of coffee, the Costa Rican government long encouraged deforestation to clear land for development by charging a lower property tax rate for clearing land. There are also a number of very small-scale coffee plantations in Costa Rica. For instance, in the small villages in the Tarrazú region, many coffee plants are grown on personal properties where the home is located, often a few inches from the house and utilized for family consumption. However, many commercial-scale plantations are built on previously forested areas. When coffee plantations are built on vegetated areas, there are three ways forests are removed: slash-and-burn, mechanical, and by hand. The slash-and-burn approach employed by many small farmers is not as productive as other approaches because key nutrients, potassium and calcium, tend to be removed from soils that are burned (Descroix 2004). Mechanical forest removal involves a combination of large equipment (e.g., bulldozers) and the use of chainsaws. Trees are felled by chainsaws then pulled offsite and the understory is bulldozed to expose the soil. Hand clearing involves using axes and chainsaws to fell trees and the understory is reduced using weed trimmers and machetes. Although mechanical or hand removal of vegetation is more energy intensive, these methods tend to leave more nutrients in the soil, particularly when the soil is not turned over with machinery. In addition, soil erosion can be reduced by leaving vegetation or using plants that are neutral or have a minimal negative effect on coffee growth. A new plantation for commercial coffee production also considers a multitude of factors that will affect production and harvest including topography, aspect, prevailing winds, and soil (Wintgens and Descroix 2012). These factors will affect how much rainfall and sunlight the site receives, if the site requires irrigation, and the ability of the soil to deliver nutrients.

The obvious ecological effect of creating a coffee plantation is that it must replace some existing habitat, and, in Costa Rica and elsewhere, this does not occur on a small-scale. According to the International Coffee Organization (https://icocoffee.org/), there were 2.7 million hectares (6.7 million acres) devoted to coffee growing in 2020. Costa Rica devotes approximately 94,000 hectares (230,000 acres) to growing coffee (Gonzalez 2020). Estimating the total area used by coffee is complicated by an ever-changing tropical landscape where abandoned ranches can convert to coffee growing only to be abandoned again (Kerr et al. 2003).

Land can be cleared mechanically, chemically, with fire, or a combination of these methods. Many plantations cut down larger trees with chainsaws and then make piles, which can be burned when dried. Burning all the vegetation is not recommended since it removes organic matter, exposes the soil, and promotes erosion, particularly on slopes (Wintgens and Descroix 2012). In flat terrain, coffee plants are planted in rows or a grid. On slopes, the land is terraced such that coffee plants grow on the flat areas while grasses or perennial plants grow on the slopes to hold the soil. Sometimes land between rows can be so steep that the feet of the coffee picker in one row are over the head of the coffee picker in the row below. Leguminous plants may also be added as ground cover before planting coffee plants to add nitrogen to the soil and prevent erosion. Only in the driest regions is bare soil practiced.

The spacing of plants is a balance between maximizing yield (harvest) and minimizing the effect of shade on neighboring plants. Since sunlight powers the growth of coffee and their fruit, shading will decrease yield. Taller varieties, therefore, require greater spacing, and varieties less tolerant of the sun will also require greater shade. Other factors that can influence the spacing of plants are soil quality, which affects water availability and competition for nutrients, and whether the plantation will be managed manually or mechanically. Arabica is typically planted 2 to 3 meters apart (Wintgens and Descroix 2012). Dwarf varieties of Arabica can be spaced much closer, which can help farmers to plant at a much higher density. Although the yield of a plantation can increase with higher density plantings, high-density plantings will pull nutrients out of the soil faster than they can be replaced, and greater amounts of fertilizers may be necessary.

In general, coffee plants maintain commercially viable yields from the fifth year to around their thirty-fifth year. However, the lifespan of the plant is reduced under intensive management of high-density plantings and varieties that grow in full sun (Harvey et al. 2021). Although the yields are initially higher, intensively managed plantations require more intervention, as coffee plants must be replaced sooner than plants using other farming techniques, namely using organic fertilizers. The inability to replace aging coffee plants will significantly impact the economic viability of a coffee farm. Farmers must use a nursery for a relatively stable yearly harvest income.

Coffee plants continuously grow, so they must be continuously pruned to keep them from shading their coffee neighbors and to keep the plants within reach for harvesting (although in Ethiopia, coffee plants are harvested by ladder and allowed to grow several meters tall). In Costa Rica, plants are maintained to be relatively round-shaped and less than 1.5 meters high. Dead and dying branches are also removed, as are any cherries from previous harvests that were missed by pickers. Additionally, pruning induces branching, so each plant becomes denser. However, a coffee plant can become dense enough that self-shading can be problematic. That is, the upper leaves can shade the lower leaves to the point that those branches no longer produce cherries and become prone to disease. The delicate balance between pruning and leaving branches requires in-depth knowledge of the life of coffee plants that comes from years of watching over a plantation.

EFFECTS OF INTENSELY MANAGED COFFEE GROWING ON BIODIVERSITY

This section is an overview of the effects of intensely managed coffee growing on various taxonomic groups, as well as providing some insight into how to study different organisms in the wild. To start, it should be no surprise that intensely managed coffee plantations have fewer trees and fewer tree species than shade and rustic coffee plantations (Philpott et al. 2008). Additionally, intensely managed coffee farms use more fertilizer and pesticides. One basic study design in ecology is to inventory an intensely managed coffee plantation and compare these results to either other types of coffee plantations or to nearby forested sites. The basic question asked in these types of studies is: Does growing coffee reduce the diversity of the taxon of interest?

Because most birds make their presence known through songs and calls, they are much easier to study, and we know much more about birds than any other taxonomic group. The effects of deforestation and coffee growing on birds are also relatively well-studied in Costa Rica (e.g., Şekercioğlu et al. 2007, 2019). Generally, we can classify the effect of coffee growing on birds into two groups: winners and losers. The winners, those that benefit from coffee plantations, tend to be species that are accustomed to disturbance and would be found in the backyard of any tropical home (Şekercioğlu et al. 2019). The losers are species that are closely tied to the complex structure found in tropical rainforests and disappear from coffee plantations, which comprise the majority of species in tropical forests. In Costa Rica, the winners are ubiquitous species such as the Tropical Kingbird (*Tyrannus melancholicus*), Blue-gray Tanager (*Thraupis episcopus*), and Clay-colored Thrush (*Turdus grayi*). These species are abundant in a variety of habitats and thrive in human-disturbed environments, including gardens, parks, and any brushy areas. The losers of deforestation far outnumber the winners and include many groups restricted to the New World tropics, such as trogons, woodcreepers, and antbirds. Antbirds are a highly diverse group that includes species that forage anywhere from the canopy to the midstory, to those that walk on the forest floor. This last group, the terrestrial insectivores, appears to be particularly sensitive to deforestation, including coffee growing (Stratford and Stouffer 1999). Ant-following birds, a taxonomically diverse assemblage of birds that specialize in feeding on invertebrates fleeing from marauding army ant swarms, are also sensitive to open areas and avoid large coffee plantations (Roberts et al. 2000).

Mammals, in particular can be difficult to study since many are nocturnal and quiet (howler monkeys are a notable exception!). Mammals can be studied through the use of live-traps, motion-activated cameras (also called camera trapping), and tracks. One recent development in the field study of mammals involves sampling DNA in insects or parasites associated with mammals. For example, Saranholi et al. (2024) used DNA in dung beetle intestines to identify Amazonian mammals. These new methods are particularly important in Central and South America, where mammals are particularly diverse (Ojeda and Novillo 2024). Despite advancements, there are far fewer studies on the effect of coffee growing on mammals than there are on birds. The few studies revealed a pattern similar to—but not exactly the same as—those of birds. Generally, coffee plantations have fewer mammal species than forests (Bedoya-Durán et al. 2023, Rocha et al., 2011). Coffee plantations with more overstory trees had fewer overall mammal species than intact forests but had larger species that may help control coffee pests (Gallina, Mandujano, and González-Romero 1996, Caudill and Rice 2016).

Reptiles and amphibians are also difficult to study. Many species of snakes, for instance, are cryptic and immobile. Studying snakes in Costa Rica and throughout the tropics involves walking transects at night and searching for the reflected eyeshine (Dorcas and Willson 2009). While a nighttime walk through a coffee plantation may seem pleasant, a nighttime hike through the Costa Rican forest comes with actual dangers, such as bumping into the incredibly (almost disturbingly) camouflaged fer-de-lance (*Bothrops asper*). Although not dangerous, many amphibians either live underground or in the treetops for most of their lives and only emerge a few times a year. Fortunately, there has been an increasing number of studies of the human impact on reptiles and amphibians since the review by Moguel and Toledo (1999). One large-scale study showed that coffee plantations maintain regional diversity, although there are lower densities compared to nearby forests (Mendenhall et al. 2014). Mendenhall's study also showed that forested riparian corridors are extremely important for maintaining diversity.

Studying tropical insects is very different from studying tropical vertebrates. Whereas most, but not all, of the ten thousand tropical vertebrates in Latin America have been named and described, there are millions of invertebrate species in the tropics, and most have not been described. How can ecologists tackle an ecological system with so many unknown species? Instead of working with named species, entomologists often work at the order and family taxonomic level. So, they may not know what species of termite they found, but they can recognize that it belongs in the termite order. This is probably adequate for many studies since insects of the same family and order often (but not always) share the same function. For example, a termite consumes woody material regardless of whether it is one species or another. This coarse-grain approach when asking questions about ecosystem services and how coffee might impact the abundance of pollinators, predatory insects, and pests. At a finer level, another method is to recognize different species by their appearance without knowing what they are. This approach uses the morphological species concept and is useful when species diversity questions are asked. Although there are millions of unknown species, there are thousands of known species in Costa Rica. It should be no surprise that the best-known species are those that are commonly encountered (e.g., leaf-cutting ants) or are impactful to humans (e.g., various mosquito species).

Tools to study tropical insects are varied and depend on the type of insect. Commonly used techniques include small colorful bowls, partially filled with soapy water, which are used to study pollinators; cups placed in the soil to capture crawling insects; and insects on plants can be captured with a sweep net. Scavenging or predatory ants and wasps are often attracted to bits of fish and meat. Lastly, some insects are studied using fogging with an insecticide, as made famous in the movie *Arachnophobia*. Escobar-Ramírez and colleagues (2020) studied ants in coffee plantations, since ants are predators of the coffee borer beetle. They discovered fewer species of ants in intensively managed coffee plantations. The effect of coffee growing on spiders is complex. Spiders are important predators of coffee pests but are also prey items to birds and lizards. Marín and Perfecto (2013) found more spiders in intensely managed coffee plantations and hypothesized that the greater abundance was due to more prey items as well as a lack of avian and lizard predators.

Together, these studies show that biodiversity is reduced when intensely managed coffee plantations supplant forests. What are the consequences of the loss of biodiversity for the coffee farmer and the larger community? One simple consequence is stepping away from the United Nations Sustainable Development Goal of "halt[ing] biodiversity loss" (https://sdgs.un.org/topics/biodiversity-and-ecosystems). But there can be consequences seen and unseen for the coffee farmer. A coffee plantation that is intensively managed may have increased yield in the short-term but there are consequences of biodiversity loss that may impair the long-term success of the plantation. For example, the loss of pest predators, primarily insectivorous birds and bats (Karp and Daily 2014), means the farmer may need to use more pesticides, which can reduce the number of pollinators. The loss of pollinators, in turn, may reduce yield (Pereira Machado et al. 2024). Pollination is one of those ecosystem services that cannot be reasonably substituted with human effort. One problem with assessing the consequences of biodiversity loss is that (1) we do not know all the species found where coffee grows, which means that (2) we cannot fully understand all the potential interactions between species that may affect coffee and (3) we do not know how climate change and invasive species will alter species interactions.

MITIGATING THE EFFECTS OF DEFORESTATION FOR COFFEE PLANTATIONS

There are a number of ways that the negative impacts of coffee growing on biodiversity can be mitigated. These approaches to offset the negative impact on coffee growing can be grouped into two broad strategies: (1) manage what happens within the plantation and (2) manage with the size or surrounding landscape of the plantation, or a combination of these strategies. The first strategy would manage the plants that grow alongside the coffee plants to promote diversity. Coffee grown under a forest canopy (aka shade-grown) is an example of the first strategy by promoting the inclusion of tall overstory trees, which provide habitat and cover for a multitude of animals as well as ferns, orchids, and other plants that live on the trees. The second strategy involves smaller plantations that are surrounded by forest. If smaller plantations are not economically viable, then a larger plantation with forested hedgerows breaking up the plantations can be used.

The first strategy takes advantage of plants being at the base of the forest food chain and acting as both a resource (e.g., leaves and fruit) as well as a substrate for foraging organisms that indirectly use plants. Not surprisingly then, the diversity of animals associated with different coffee-growing methods is closely tied to plant diversity. For arthropods, rustic and traditional polycultures in Mexico had biological communities similar to cultivated forests of similar climates (Moguel and Toledo 1999). In addition, there were few reports of pests from these types of plantations, which they attributed to high populations of predators, such as spiders and ants. In Mexico, Moguel and Toledo (1999) reported that bird species increased with increasing forest complexity from the lowest in sun coffee to the highest in rustic farms. Some of the diversity is dependent on the context of the plantation, with sites surrounded by forest having more species than plantations in other contexts. Shaded plantations also supported many more migrating birds than other types of plantations. It is not just the trees per se that are important. By removing epiphytes from shade trees in experimental plots, Cruz-Angón and Greenberg (2005) were able to show that there were fewer forest bird species in the experimental plots than in plots where epiphytes were left on trees. Many of the birds in the Cruz-Angón and Greenberg (2005) study were insectivores, and Cruz-Angón et al. (2009) showed that epiphytes increased the abundance and diversity of arthropods.

The rainforest where coffee grows, particularly in the New World, has a predictable structure. Recreating that structure is the key to maximizing diversity. Going from bottom to top begins with the epigeal layer that is just above the soil. The epigeal layer is composed of leaves in various states of decay, from newly fallen leaves to the duff, where small leaf particles are intermixed with roots and soil. Mixed into the leaf litter are fungi and various invertebrates that are breaking down the leaves, as well as vertebrate and invertebrate predators of those organisms. Depending on light availability, there might be a thin layer of non-woody plants, including ferns. This lowest layer of plants can be relatively thin because there may be very little light reaching this layer. Moving up in the forest is the shrub layer that contains both woody and non-woody plants, such as various tall grasses. This layer of the forest is the most difficult to recreate in a coffee plantation. The primary reason is that too much light reaches the ground, which promotes the growth of herbaceous plants, such as grasses. Since the goal of a coffee plantation is to grow coffee, there is likely very little that can be done to address this, as coffee does require more light than a closed canopy allows. Another reason a typical forest floor cannot be recreated in most coffee plantations is that there is not a complex leaf litter layer that supports an invertebrate community that, in turn, supports the epigeal insectivores that rely on them. Only in the most rustic plantations is there a leaf litter layer resembling anything close to an undisturbed forest. This likely explains why there are so few terrestrial insectivorous birds, as noted by several studies (e.g., Stratford and Stouffer 1999). If mulch is applied, it is usually grass clippings or coffee processing waste, such as the spent cherries. Although these are not ideal for wildlife, they are an improvement over bare ground, which is prone to erosion, dries out more quickly, and supports less diversity.

The next layer up from the leaf litter layer is the shrub layer. Woody plants of the shrub layer include multi-stemmed palms, young trees, and various shrubs. The midstory is composed of younger trees and the trunks of canopy trees. In a typical coffee plantation, the shrub layer is composed entirely of coffee plants. Above the shrub layer is the midstory. In the undisturbed rainforest, this is occupied by a few palm trees and younger trees. In the native ranges of *C. arabica* and *C. canephora*, where plants may not be trimmed, coffee plants may even grow high into the midstory. Finally, above the midstory is the canopy. The canopy is the top layer of the forest and can be dense enough to intercept most of the light. In lowland tropical forests, the canopy can be dense enough to support such animals as the tamandua, a small Neotropical anteater that can move from tree to tree by simply walking from branch to branch. The canopy in lowland forests is typically between 25–35 m. Emergent trees poke through the canopy and can be 40 m. Because soils on slopes tend to be less stable, such huge emergent trees are rare on hillsides. A typical Costa Rican coffee plantation has plants that would be of similar stature to the midstory. There are only the occasional large trees in plantations and these are typically in the margins of the plantation. Most coffee plantations that we have observed have been shaded monocultures (sensu Moguel and Toledo 1999).

The midstory, canopy, and emergent trees are hosts to a number of epiphytes—plants that grow on other trees. Rainforest epiphytes include vines that grow from the ground up or from the canopy down, mosses, ferns, lichens, orchids, and more. A higher density of epiphytes can be supported where it is more humid, such as montane forests and alongside rivers. Indeed, epiphytes can be so dense in some locations that the trunk and branch of the tree are not visible. In areas that are drier, such as the Pacific slope of the Talamanca mountains, trees do not have such a high density of epiphytes, but epiphytic bromeliads are common. This complexity of vegetation supports the most diverse biota on the planet. The effects of coffee farming on biodiversity will depend on various factors, but mostly the choice of shading and the choice of shade trees. Generally speaking, the more that the tree canopy is removed, the greater the loss of biodiversity.

THROWING SHADE AT SUN COFFEE

Of all the layers of the forest that affect diversity within a coffee plantation, the canopy layer appears to be the most important. Not only do trees affect diversity, but trees and their cover affect several aspects of plantation management, including how much pesticide and fertilizer is used. Shade also affects the lifespan of individual coffee plants and coffee yield (Descroix 2004). Coffee plantations are not necessarily shade or sun. Rather, the amount of shade is a continuum from no canopy over coffee to a closed canopy formed from the leaves and branches over a coffee plant. At one end of the shade spectrum is sun coffee, which includes a dense monoculture of coffee plants. Sun coffee does not have any overstory trees, and yields are

Table 3.1 The Relationship between How Plantations Are Managed in Respect to Tree Cover and the Consequences for Biodiversity, Yield, Fertilizer, and Pesticide Use, and the Lifespan of Individual Coffee Plants

Plantation Type	*Biodiversity*	*Yield*	*Fertilizer Intensity*	*Pesticide Intensity*	*Lifespan of Individual Coffee Plants*
Sun	Lowest	Highest	High	Widely used	Shortest
Partial shade	Low	High	High	Variable	Short
Shade	Medium	Medium	Low	Variable	Long
Rustic	Highest	Lowest	None	None or selected trees	Longest

Source: Generated by the Authors

generally high (table 3.1). Most sun coffee plantations are Robusta plants, which are more tolerant of high temperatures and direct sun. Sun coffee also has high yields at the expense of having high inputs of synthetic fertilizers and pesticides (Moguel and Toledo 1999). Generally, sun coffee has low biodiversity because the coffee plants themselves provide little habitat for birds and other organisms. Sun coffee is not common in Costa Rica since most plantations are growing Arabica coffee.

Providing slightly more habitat are shaded monocultures. These plantations only have coffee in the understory but have a sparse overstory of trees. Many of these trees are continually coppiced to reduce their shade to a desired low level. In Costa Rica, we have observed these commercial shaded monocultures (sensu Moguel and Toledo 1999) with relatively sparse plantings of *Musa* varieties (banana) and *Inga*. Shaded monocultures may provide similar shade to commercial polycultures, but other useful plants are mixed in with the coffee. *Inga* is a popular choice of shade tree since it does have symbiotic nitrogen-fixing bacteria, the fruits can be eaten, and the canopy is lower and wider—making this species easier to manage. *Inga* is easily recognizable as most species have large (> 20 cm) seed pods hanging from branches. The flowers of *Inga* are attractive to invertebrate and avian pollinators, such as orioles and hummingbirds. Even though the trees are kept short-statured, they commonly have epiphytes, such as bromeliads, that further increase the diversity of plants and the organisms that interact with them. Commercial polyculture is structurally similar to shaded monoculture, but the understory is a mix of coffee and other crops, such as citrus, bananas, and beans.

The most shaded coffee plantations are those classified as rustic and traditional polyculture (Moguel and Toledo 1999). These plantations have a dense and high canopy over the coffee plants, which are often mixed with other crops. These plantations are structurally the closest to rainforests and have the highest diversity of organisms. The trees in shade coffee plantations in Chiapas, Mexico, were dominated by native tree species (Soto-Pinto et al. 2001). The non-native species in Chiapas were mostly fruit trees (e.g., *Inga*). Rustic and traditional polycultures (sensu Moguel and Toledo 1999) support numerous epiphytes, including orchids, and the shade trees were useful to farmers as well.

One of the premier designations of shade-grown coffee is the Smithsonian's Bird-Friendly certification. In addition to being certified as organic, for a farm to be considered Bird-Friendly, it must meet a number of criteria (https://nationalzoo.si.edu/migratory-birds/bird-friendly-farm-criteria) that are primarily related to adding tall trees and shrubs of different species to the plantation. Bird-Friendly certification also requires herbaceous plants beneath coffee plants as well as some leaf litter. As the Smithsonian notes (https://nationalzoo.si.edu/migratory-birds/ecological-benefits-shade-grown-coffee), there are numerous ecological benefits to adding structural and taxonomic diversity to the coffee plantation.

Although the classifications are useful, there is a smooth gradient between sun coffee and rustic plantations. Moreover, shade is a dynamic feature of a plantation as the rainy season comes and goes, branches fall off due to disease and weather, and plantation managers trim trees. There is a delicate balance when it comes to fungal diseases and selecting the amount of shade. Too little shade can reduce brown eye spot disease (*Cercospora* coffeicola), but too much shade can benefit American leaf spot *(Mycena citricolor*) disease and coffee leaf rust (*H. vastatrix*).

Market forces, desire for certifications, local conditions, and diseases will determine the density of shade trees, as well as the mix of plants in the plantation. In Costa Rica, for instance, there was a drive to intensify coffee production in the early 1970s to the point where most coffee plantations would be considered sun or mostly sun coffee with intensive use of pesticides and fertilizers (Castro-Tanzi et al. 2012). Overall, about half of all Latin American coffee farms are high intensity (Harvey et al. 2021). There is also land use pressure on coffee plantations from other agricultural products as well, such as beef production, which is one of the most important competitors to coffee production.

Toward the rustic plantation side, shade coffee plantations have an overstory of native or mostly native trees, and the canopy can reach heights of 30–40 meters. Farmers may choose to replace native trees with species that may provide added economic or home use, such as rubber (*Castilla elastica*) and several species of *Inga* (Moguel and Toledo 1999).

MANAGING SOIL AND NUTRIENTS

Soil conservation is a key component of ecological sustainability and is an important issue in nearly all agricultural systems (Borrelli et al. 2021). Sustainable coffee farming involves practices that reduce soil erosion and make the land arable in the future. In particular, sustainable coffee farming aims to avoid soil acidification resulting from excess nitrogen applications.

There are three primary soils in the tropics, and these make all the difference in how coffee is grown. Over huge swaths of the Amazon rainforest and other lowland areas are Oxisols and Ultisols. These are highly weathered soils that are generally nutrient-poor and are generally not productive in the long-term without significant inputs of fertilizers. The lush growth of the Amazonian forest is dependent on the efficient cycling of nutrients from the decomposition of other organisms. Although the tropical climate of the Amazon basin is appropriate for coffee, the soils make sustainable coffee growing in this region a challenge. This was well known by the indigenous peoples of the Amazon region, who created pockets of highly productive soils through the systematic use of mulching organic material into the soil. In strong contrast to the nutrient-poor Ultisols and Oxisols are the Andisols of Costa Rica, Colombia, and a number of other highland sites. Andisols are nutrient-rich soils of volcanic origin that are well-drained, well-aerated, and have a pH that is ideal for coffee plants.

The volcanic activity that created the productive Costa Rican hillsides also makes the soils prone to erosion. Reducing erosion to preserve soil is incredibly important to the long-term soil health of coffee plantations. In addition to using plants to help against soil erosion, it can be reduced by strategies such as contour planting and bench terracing. Both of these approaches have stacks of flat rows where coffee is grown with slopes between the coffee rows. Vetiver, dense rows of herbaceous plants between rows also helps reduce erosion. Fallen tree leaves, weeds, and other plant material can be left on the plantation to promote soil organic matter. Organic matter serves as a nutrient source and can also reduce water evaporation from the soil surface (Snoeck and Vaast 2004). Coffee plantations that manage their soils can not only contribute to the long-term soil health of the plantation but can help the watershed with flooding issues. Unlike sugar cane and land used as cattle pasture, which have compacted soils, coffee plantations are much more like forests in terms of their ability to hold water and prevent soil runoff (Toohey et al. 2018).

In addition to soil erosion, soil acidification is another potential issue with coffee farming. Plants, including coffee, often have a narrow range of pH (the shorthand for referring to the acidity of a substance). The ideal pH for coffee is just slightly acidic and the andisols of Costa Rica naturally are ideal. However, the excess application of nitrogen to soils can lower pH and make it more acidic. Even modest decreases in pH can result in lower coffee yields (Zhao et al. 2018) and may also make the plants more susceptible to fungal pests (Castro-Tanzi et al. 2012). Soil acidification can take several years to naturally remediate or requires the addition of lime (Castro et al. 2012), adding to the costs of managing the plantation. Fortunately, for Costa Rican coffee farmers, large inputs of nitrogen fertilizers are not necessary. However, in the lowland areas on the Caribbean slope, soils are becoming increasingly acidic where other crops, such as pineapple, are grown (Sherman and Brye 2019).

Nitrogen fertilization is required where nitrogen is depleted in the soil faster than it is replenished. For example, over 33 kilograms of nitrogen are removed from a plantation for every ton of coffee cherries harvested (Snoeck and Lambot 2012). Although nitrogen makes up most of the atmospheric gases, it is unavailable to coffee plants—as it is for most of the life on the planet. Bacteria are able to take atmospheric nitrogen and turn it into a form that is available for other bacteria in a process called nitrogen fixation. Fixed nitrogen is converted to nitrates by nitrifying bacteria, and nitrates are used by plants or are released back into the atmosphere by another group of bacteria. When plants or their parts die, their nitrogen is cycled back to the nitrifying bacteria and so on. This cycle involves many more organisms than outlined here. For example, when a leaf falls on the ground, it is not immediately available to nitrifying bacteria. Instead, a host of fungi and invertebrates break the leaf down to its basic components. Some of the organic matter of the leaf becomes part of the soil as well.

If farmers want to minimize using fertilizers, then leguminous plants should be encouraged. Leguminous plants are primarily in the family Fabaceae, which are associated with bacteria that have the amazing ability to convert atmospheric nitrogen into a form that plants can use. These plants include clovers, beans, peas, soy, peanuts, and a host of non-domesticated species that are useful as cover crops. One commonly used nitrogen-fixing tree is Inga. This genus of tree has many species that produce long pods with a deliciously sweet inner lining.

Another alternative to the application of nitrogen fertilizer is mulch. Mulch is nonliving plant material, such as wood chips, leaves, and grasses, added to the surface or near the surface of the soil. Adding mulch between coffee plants is standard for most plantations, as it reduces erosion, controls weeds, buffers temperature changes throughout the day, and provides a suite of nutrients to the soil. The nutrients in mulch become available as bacteria, fungi, and invertebrates break down the plant material. Typically, a small ring is kept clear directly around the base of the plant to reduce humidity and fungal infections at the base.

There are a number of reasons why farmers may choose to use synthetic fertilizers as an alternative to or in addition to mulch. One, nitrogen and other nutrients take time to become available to the coffee plants, and the amount of nutrients may be insufficient to offset the nutrients that are removed from the soil by the plants. Two, the amount of nutrients available in mulch is not as predictable as synthetic fertilizers—which are printed on the bags. Part of the uncertainty in the amount of nutrients in mulch results from the varying sources of mulch. In plantations that have an overstory of trees, mulch may simply be sourced from the leaves of those trees in addition to leaves dropped from the coffee plant. Other plantations will use grasses off the site or herbaceous plants that grow between rows and die during the dry season. A growing trend is to use the remains of the cherry, such as the pulp and parchment, that are removed from the bean during processing. However, waste material is usually composted for some time before being applied to a field.

There are many benefits to the use of mulch, such as the reduction of soil erosion from the mulching of shade tree leaves, and the variation in soil and air temperatures is reduced (Descroix 2004). Moreover, shade trees and their fallen leaves intercept rain and reduce the effects of heavy rains on bare soil. There are, of course, disadvantages to having shade trees, including competition for soil moisture, reduced productivity, and maintenance of the shade trees. Moguel and Toledo (1999) note that coffee farms in Mexico under heavy shade are also associated with more indigenous peoples but have a lower yield. However, Soto-Pinto et al. (2001) found no differences in yield between the amount of yield and the amount of shade. Maintenance of shade trees includes pruning since trees will grow to fill empty spaces in the canopy. The recommended shade for coffee is somewhere between 30 percent and 70 percent depending on local conditions (Wintgens and Descroix 2012). Plants are prone to diseases outside of this range and productivity (Muschler 2004). In Central America, coffee was largely grown in the shade, but larger crops were encouraged by markets and governmental programs (Muschler 2004). The choice of shading is determined by several economic factors. Generally, the less shade, the higher the yield (Schmitt et al. 2010), and the greater the likelihood that the coffee is going to a wider market. The exceptions are niche markets, such as bird-friendly coffees.

The nutrients that are typically included in fertilizer are nitrogen, phosphorus, and potassium. Nutrients required in smaller amounts include zinc, aluminum, calcium, magnesium, manganese, copper, sulfur, and boron. Mulch can also provide these nutrients, albeit with the same issues as nitrogen. Despite having lower yield, shade coffee provides mulch naturally as leaves drop from the overstory trees. Although yield is lower, coffee grown under shade is presumably higher quality (Muschler 2004). Therefore, sun coffee is often more profitable in the short-term, but long-term soil conservation would benefit from the use of some shade.

PEST MANAGEMENT

Coffee pests are organisms that reduce the productivity of a coffee plantation and include various animals that harm coffee plants and plants that compete with coffee for light, nutrients, and water. Plants that are pests are simply called weeds. Though mulch and shade trees can reduce the problem, weeds will need to be controlled. Coffee growers can use hand tools, mowing, plastic sheeting, or herbicides to remove weeds, depending on budget and whether the farmer wants to be certified organic, which forbids the use of synthetic herbicides. Some weeds might be desirable, such as legumes that are associated with nitrogen-fixing bacteria. Additionally, some farmers may allow strips of weeds between coffee plants as a measure for soil control.

Shade trees may also reduce the effect of invertebrate pests directly and indirectly. Jaramillo and colleagues (2011) suggest that the reduced temperatures provided by shade trees could reduce the effects of increased temperatures on the coffee borer beetle, which can increase the number of generations with rising temperatures. Indirectly, but no less importantly, shade trees provide habitat for birds, including insectivorous birds that forage on coffee pests. Working in central Kenya, Kammerichs-Berke and colleagues (2022) found that plantations shaded by native trees in the genus Cordia had more insectivorous birds, more prey for insectivorous birds, and were cooler than plantations shaded by non-native *Grevillea robusta* trees. In Costa Rica, Martínez-Salinas and colleagues found that the functional diversity of birds was negatively associated with borer-beetle abundance. In other words, the more types of birds, the fewer the borer beetles.

Nematodes, also called roundworms, are highly diverse and incredibly abundant animals that primarily live in the soil. Ecologically, they are diverse as well and have a wide range of sizes and ecological functions. Many nematodes are predators of bacteria and other soil microorganisms, and a number of species predate other nematodes. The species that cause problems for the coffee industry are those that are parasitic on the roots of the coffee plant. These parasitic species consume carbohydrates from the plant, which means that the plant has fewer resources for itself or for beneficial symbiotic species. Nematodes may physically damage roots and cause the plant to grow less efficient roots. Nematodes also have a wide range of effects depending on the nematode species, the coffee species and variety, as well as a number of mitigating factors such as soil moisture and plantation management. Resistant varieties of Arabica include Typica, Mundo Novo, and Bourbon, and most varieties of Robusta are resistant (Castillo and Wintgens 2004). The effects of the nematode include wilting, reduced berry yield, death, and a shortened lifespan. Pesticides are used on large plantations to treat infected plants and grafting from susceptible Arabica onto resistant Robusta rootstock can also be effective.

Fungi are organisms that are often classified as plants but are more closely related to animals. Fungi have a dazzling array of enzymes that are involved in nutrient cycling. Along with bacteria, fungi are essential for the breakdown of dead organic matter into components that are used by themselves and other organisms, including coffee. The literature is replete with examples of fungi that form close symbiotic relationships with plants. Plants provide the products of photosynthesis, carbohydrates, and fungi provide nutrients to the plants. Not all fungal-plant interactions are positive. There are a number of economically important fungi that cause damage to coffee plants. The most important fungal pest is coffee leaf rust (*Hemileia vastatrix*). This fungus invades the layer of the coffee leaf where photosynthesis occurs and reduces the amount of energy available to the plant. The most common effects of *H. vastatrix* are reduced yield and leaf drop, but infections can be bad enough to cause death. Like other pathogens, varieties differ in their susceptibility and pathogenicity, and the intensity of infections can vary geographically. Leaf rust can also be the result of local conditions. Shrubs that are too dense may be susceptible, as well as plants that have too much shade. Treatment for coffee leaf rust is primarily copper-containing fungicides that are applied by spray directly to leaves.

There are a number of other pathogenic fungi, but these tend to be more localized. A number of rusts other than coffee leaf rust affect coffee plants and there are other fungi that attach to the trunk of the tree. Most of these fungi are associated with damaged plants or individual plants that receive too much or too little shade, depending on their variety. These localized occurrences can usually be corrected by changing practices on the site, such as pruning and altering the amount of shade. Similarly, there are few bacterial or viral diseases that affect coffee production, and these tend to have localized outbreaks. One exception is coffee ringspot virus, but for now, this pathogen is only a problem in Brazil (Kitajima and Chagas 2004).

The tropics have a remarkable diversity of insects. There are, perhaps, millions of species of beetles, wasps, flies, true bugs, and other groups. Few of these insects are pests of coffee since coffee has an array of chemicals used for defense. Indeed, the evolution of plant defenses may have played a role in the evolution of so many insect species. Some insect pests consume the leaf, including the coffee leaf miner *(Leucoptera coffeella*). This tiny moth lays an egg on the coffee leaf and the young caterpillar grows as it chews its way through the leaf's mesophyll—the middle layer of the leaf that is less protected than the two outer dermal layers. The coffee leaf miner is a problem in Puerto Rico and has not been a problem in Costa Rica or other coffee-growing regions (Perfecto et al. 2021). Another consumer of coffee leaves is the leaf-cutter ant (*Atta cephalotes*). This species very efficiently cuts leaves into tiny pieces, which are then carried to an underground nest that contains a fungus that consumes the leaves the ants deliver to it. This relationship is somewhat offset by the fact that the ants improve the soil (García-Cárdenas et al. 2022).

The most important insect pest in the Americas is the coffee borer beetle (*Hypothenemus hampei*). This tiny beetle burrows through the outer layer of the green coffee cherry to the bean, where a female lays an egg. The developing larva consumes the bean, making it unfit for coffee. The larva develop in the bean and emerge to mate and infect more coffee cherries. Most of the infected beans are selected out during processing, reducing the yield. The coffee borer beetle is native to Africa and has become a serious pest throughout the world, including Central and South America (Cure et al. 2020). Up to 95 percent of berries on an individual plant can be infected (Marino et al. 2017). Local populations of the beetle can be reduced by stripping, which involves complete removal of all fruits during a harvest, combined with the removal of fallen fruit. Several parasitoid wasps lay eggs on the developing borer larvae, and the parasitoid consumes the beetle larvae in the coffee bean. These parasitoids reduce the population of larvae but less so than stripping. Stripping also removes the developing wasps, so these two approaches are incompatible with each other (Cure et al. 2020).

Parasites of coffee pests include several species of wasps that use insect bodies as food for developing young. Invertebrate predators include predacious ants, beetles, lacewings, and many more. In addition to insectivorous birds, bats and lizards are known to consume coffee pests. Ants, particularly arboreal species, prey on both the coffee leaf miner (*Leucoptera coffeella*) and the coffee borer beetle (*Hypothenemus hampei*). One complicating issue is that potential coffee predators can have an effect on each other. Perfecto and colleagues (2021) studied an interesting case in Puerto Rico. There, anoline lizards, common in the pet trade, are effective at controlling the coffee leaf miner. However, an introduced species of ant, *Wasmannia auropunctata*, has a negative effect on the lizards and, consequently, has a positive effect on the coffee leaf miner. In Mexico, the ant *Azteca instabilis* (Perfecto and Vandermeer 2006) forms a symbiotic relationship with the scale insect *Coccus viridis.* Though the scale insect sucks on the phloem of the coffee plants, the presence of the *Azteca* ants reduces the number of coffee borer beetles (Perfecto and Vandermeer 2006).

These complex interactions indicate that invasive species and distribution changes due to climate change are likely to have unforeseen consequences that are likely negative for coffee production. Moreover, there is likely to be geographic variation in the effect of these interactions on coffee yield. For example, shade trees had no effect on natural predation in an Indian coffee plantation (Sinu et al., 2021).

Birds generate their own body heat, which has higher fuel requirements than ectotherms such as lizards and insects. To fuel their metabolic needs, many birds require constant foraging during their waking hours. This can make insectivorous birds effective invertebrate predators, even more so when birds are feeding young. By removing phytophagous insects that are eating plant leaves, birds can increase plant growth. Ecologists are now at the point where they can quantify the effect of birds on plant growth. Marquis and Whelan (1994) netted young white oaks to exclude birds and compared them to oaks that were accessed by birds. Netted white oaks had more leaf-damaging insects and grew more slowly. Since this seminal study, numerous other studies have shown the beneficial effects of birds on plants, including understory trees in hardwood forests (Schwenk, Strong, and Sillett 2010), desert plants (Bang, Faeth, and Sabo 2012), and tropical trees (Van Bael, Brawn, and Robinson 2003). Experiments in agricultural systems also show birds are effective predators and increase the yield of crop plants, such as Brassica (Hooks, Pandey, and Johnson 2003), in Californian (Jedlicka, Greenberg, and Letourneau 2011) and Chilean vineyards (Rodríguez-San Pedro et al. 2020), and cocoa (Van Bael, Bichier, and Greenberg 2007). Not surprisingly, birds have been shown to be important in reducing insect pests in coffee plantations (Karp et al. 2013, Maas et al. 2016). What is surprising is that birds are effective in reducing coffee borer beetle infestations (Johnson, Kellermann, and Stercho 2010, Kellermann et al. 2008). In other agricultural systems, the focus was on larger folivorous insects, primarily caterpillars. The studies on birds and borer beetles are remarkable because borer beetles are much tinier. More recent research has shown the positive effect of bats on agricultural productivity (Karp and Daily 2014, Maas et al. 2016). Given that the leaf miner moth is nocturnal, bats are likely helping coffee by reducing this pest, but more research is needed.

To exploit natural predators, the abundance and diversity of birds, bats, wasps, spiders, and lizards should be maximized when possible. Like pollination services, nearby forests and shade trees promote diversity in coffee plantations (Bedoya-Durán et al. 2023). The few species that forage in sun coffee in Central America are the species that will have less impact on coffee than the more specialist species found in the forest. Shade trees increase avian diversity in coffee plantations. Bird diversity is also increased with small patches of forest, rather than in hedgerows (Munoz et al. 2013). One interesting aspect of shade coffee, particularly in Central America, is the importance of coffee plantations to long-distance migrant birds that breed in North America and spend the Northern Hemisphere winters in Central America. Many of these long-distance migrants found in coffee plantations are small-bodied insectivores. Because they are consuming insects and we are providing a habitat for them, this is a good example of a mutually beneficial relationship. Since coffee plantations are easily accessible, there is a growing trend of bird tourism in the tropics (Şekercioğlu 2012). Not only does this increase awareness of the importance of shade trees for birds, but can bring extra incentives for coffee farmers by increasing the revenue from a plantation.

MANAGING POLLINATORS

Pollination is the movement of pollen from the pollen-producing anthers to the ovary-containing pistil. One of the more remarkable aspects of pollination is that the pollen-receiving structure, the stigma, is capable of recognizing not only different species but relatedness of the pollen that has landed on its surface. The stigma can then either accept the pollen and allow a pollen tube to reach the ovary, or the plant can reject the pollen. Selfing, or self-pollination, refers to plants that can use their own pollen to fertilize. Outcrossing refers to fertilization by pollination from other individuals. Though the difference between selfing and outcrossing may seem insignificant, there are several important short-term considerations for the farmer and for the long-term sustainability of the industry. Outcrossing increases genetic diversity within a population, which is a key feature of adaptation and surviving climate change and pests. The drawback to genetic variation in coffee is the unpredictability of the product.

Robusta plants are obligate outcrossers, meaning that to produce fruit, Robusta plants must be planted with other non-cloned individuals (Klein et al. 2003). Not surprisingly then, Robusta plants are, pun intended, more robust to climate variability as well as pests. Arabica, in contrast, is able to both self-pollinate and outcross. Self-crossing, reduces genetic variability but increases the predictability of the coffee plants and beans produced. Thus, a farmer needs to weigh the benefits and costs of outcrossing and selfing for their own needs.

One facet of pollination in coffee is clear: since fruits are the products of fertilization, the number of fruits on a plant is, in part, driven by the number of successful pollination events. Therefore, yield, not necessarily quality, is maximized when pollination is maximized. Coffee plants are pollinated by wind, insects, or, in selfing species, by the proximity of anthers and stigmas to each other in the same flower. Selfing and wind pollination are largely out of the control of the farmer. Insect pollination, however, can be enhanced or inhibited by the farmer's decisions.

Many crops, including coffee, benefit from having a diversity of pollinators. The most popular pollinator is the honey bee (*Apis mellifera*) but there is a remarkable diversity of potential pollinators, and wild pollinators are at least as important as honey bees (Garibaldi et al. 2013). Knowing the increased yield associated with insect pollination, sustainable coffee growing should maximize the diversity of coffee pollinators. Using a modeling approach, Imbach et al. (2017) suggest that pollinator diversity can help offset reduced yields from heat stress in future warming models. There are social and nonsocial bees that are potential coffee pollinators, as well as numerous fly species. Their conservation relies on having nearby nesting places. This can include undisturbed soils for ground-nesting bees, dead trees and limbs for species that nest in tree hollows or the ends of hollow twigs, and a variety of other plant materials. Having forests adjacent to coffee plantations is an effective way to provide nesting sites. Forests need to be close enough that pollinators can reach plants. In Southeast Asia, Priess and colleagues (2007) modeled the economic loss from decreased yield with increasing distance from forests. Sustainable coffee growing may include small patches of forests within plantations to act as pollinator reservoirs, but this idea needs further research.

HARVESTING AND PROCESSING COFFEE

Due to the nature of how coffee ripens and the terrain used for coffee plantations, practically all coffee is hand-harvested. There are two general approaches to hand harvesting. One is called selective hand harvesting, which only selects the ripest cherries. This is the most common type of hand harvesting and requires multiple harvests since the coffee cherries ripen periodically throughout the season, which is normally from October to March. The second type of hand harvesting is called stripping and occurs where the ripening period is shorter, labor costs are prohibitive, or most likely at the end of the season when workers are stripping the plant of all its coffee cherries because the removal of all the cherries initiates the next round of flowering. Hand harvesting collects cherries on plastic sheeting on the ground or in baskets secured at the waist. In coffee fields that are flatter with fewer obstacles, mechanical removal of cherries is done by a pulled or self-driven harvester that shakes the shrubs and collects the fallen fruit. Mechanical harvesters take advantage of ripened fruit being dislodged more easily than unripe fruit. Harvesters are restricted to areas that are not too steep, such as much of Costa Rican plantations, or where plants are too dense. A small number of plantations employ handheld harvesting machines that have vibrating heads mounted on a pole (see Brando 2012). These handheld harvesters are powered by backpack compressors or through a hose connected to a stationary compressor.

After harvesting, cherries are separated from impurities, such as leaves, rocks, and sticks, by manual or mechanical winnowing. Winnowing involves moving the cherries over grates of different sizes and using airflow to remove unwanted materials. Cherries are then floated to separate less ripe beans with high moisture content (which sink in water) from riper beans with low moisture content (which float in water). After separation based on moisture content, the cherries are ready for processing.

There are three primary ways to process the cherries: dry, wet, and intermediate. In dry processing, the cherry is dried intact, then the bean is isolated from the outer layers mechanically. Wet processing removes the majority of pulp first; then, the mucilage and parchment are removed in a second process. Beans with the parchment are dried before the parchment is removed.

Most Arabica beans utilize wet processing (Brando 2012), and it is usually considered the optimal processing procedure to create high-quality coffee. A small number of processors use drums or discs with slots for pulping or a screen. The cherries are squeezed, and the pressure causes a bean to be exuded. Beans from ripe cherries will be squeezed out from this pressure but will contain a small amount of mucilage and the parchment around the bean. The mucilage can be removed by repeated passes or second passes that apply more pressure to the beans, causing them to rub against each other. Many mills utilize machinery devoted to removing mucilage. Some processors choose to use dry or wet fermentation to remove mucilage, often with the addition of yeast. Lastly, mills may choose to use a multitude of processes that include a short fermentation period followed by mechanized mucilage removal.

Wet milling also includes water flow in the process of removing the pulp and mucilage, so one of the outputs is water with pulp material. Processors that seek sustainable practices are attempting to engineer machines that can process cherries with less water. Many processors are also recycling water by pooling wastewater in a settling tank. Pulp and mucilage settle out in these pools, and the overlying water can be reused. Commercial pulping machines are powered by electricity or diesel. Only very small family farms use hand-powered milling machines.

The intermediate process leaves the mucilage on the parchment to dry before isolating the bean. In Costa Rica, this purportedly produces a sweeter "honey coffee." Most coffees remove the pulp using abrasion. A small number of processors use fermentation to remove the mucilage.

Another source of nutrients that can be used on a plantation to promote sustainable goals is the product of vermicomposting. In vermicomposting, worms are used to break down the by-products of coffee production. The largest byproduct of coffee production is the pulp (Aranda, Duran, and Escamilla 2004). The traditional approach to handling pulp is to dump it into or near rivers. Worms convert the pulp into products that are more available to plants. Worm castings can then be used to fertilize coffee and other crops. Most of the pulp is converted into carbon dioxide, but for every one ton of pulp, 250 kg of fertilizer is produced (Aranda, Duran, and Escamilla 2004, Flores-Solórzano et al. 2022). Some of the larger coffee operations in Costa Rica process vermicomposted coffee pulp via their own supply of worms. Usually, farmers will bring the coffee pulp from processing, which will be placed on top of the worms that eat their way to the top, creating fertilizer. Once the worms reach the top, the fertilizer is bagged; the worms then go back to the bottom, and the process begins again. This system benefits farmers by giving them a steady supply of organic fertilizer so they can maintain their certification for organic production and are normally given a discount on purchasing the final product if they contributed used coffee pulp to the project.

Coffee needs to be dried before storage. Too wet, and fungus will grow on the beans. Too dry, beans become brittle. Ideally, beans have about 12 percent moisture content. To get to this point, coffee processors use sun or machine drying. Sun drying either takes place on a large flat cement block (a patio) or on a mesh. The beans are spread out on the surface then turned periodically to keep exposure uniform. Beans that were wet-milled with the pulp and mucilage removed will take about a week to dry, and whole cherries will take about a week to dry. There are numerous arrangements for machine drying but all involve exposing the beans to hot air. Machine drying speeds up the process of drying and can also make for more consistent drying, but machine drying requires an energy source such as wood, gas, or diesel. Coffee milling by-products, such as parchment, are increasingly used to reduce waste. One common example of a machine dryer in Costa Rica is the rotary dryer. Hot air is forced up through a screened wheel. Dry or wet-milled beans are placed on top of the wheel, and a bar rotates around the wheel, mixing the coffee beans. Also common in Costa Rica is to use a mixture of drying techniques.

Once beans are dried, hulling will remove the remaining layers. Wet-milled beans will only have parchment around the bean, intermediate milled beans will have mucilage and parchment, and dry-milled beans will have all the layers of cherry—albeit with most of the water removed. These other layers are removed with machine hulling, which involves moving beans against each other or a rough surface. This process also polishes the beans. Fans are used to separate clean beans from the waste material. Beans are then mechanically separated by size, color, and density. Before bagging, coffee beans are bulked (similar beans put together) or blended (similar beans or beans of different origins put together).

There are a number of targets for energy conservation and sustainability in coffee processing. One area that is of interest to coffee sustainability is the diversion of pulp from being dumped into waterways. Cherry pulp is 4–12 percent protein, 1–2 percent lipid, 6–10 percent lipid, 45–89 percent carbohydrates and contains caffeine and phenols. Pulp can be used to make jams, jellies, and juices or turned into flour for breads and cookies (Murthy and Naidu 2012, Klingel et al. 2020).

Another target of sustainability is energy usage, particularly in pulp and mucilage removal and the drying of beans (Arce et al. 2009). Some processors burn firewood to supplement sun drying, exacerbating the effect of the coffee industry on tropical forests (Arce et al. 2009). To alleviate the demand for wood, some coffee processors are exploring the use of solar energy and biofuels, while others use the coffee parchment that has been removed from green coffee for roasting.

COFFEE STORAGE AND SHIPMENT

Where coffee is grown, there is a harvest season that is typically shorter than the constant demand for coffee. The result is a temporary excess of coffee and the necessity to store coffee before it can be processed. Green coffee beans are stored in bags in warehouses, for which the standard size is 60 kilograms, with some larger bags that contain 0.5–2 metric tons. The influence of green coffee storage on coffee quality cannot be overstated because, even though the exterior layers of the cherry have been stripped away, the green coffee bean is still alive. This means that the embryo in the bean is metabolizing the carbohydrates, absorbing oxygen, and emitting carbon dioxide. This should not be surprising since humans mimic the same process that the beans go through in their native range when they pass through the digestive system of birds or mammals and defecate to become the next generation of coffee plants.

Coffee in storage declines in quality, so conditions that slow the bean's metabolism are preferred. This includes lower relative humidity and lower temperatures. In Costa Rica, more ideal conditions are found at the higher altitudes where Arabica is grown. There, coffee can be stored for up to a year in well-ventilated warehouses. Storage conditions also affect pest populations. The coffee borer beetle (*H. hampei*), coffee bean weevil (*Araecerus fasciculatus*), and other invertebrate pests prefer beans that are kept at higher humidity levels.

Chapter 4

Future Biological Threats and Opportunities

CLIMATE AND COFFEE

As a country that still depends on the export of agricultural goods such as coffee, climate change has altered the way in which these goods can be produced. Biogeographers describe an organism's climate envelope, which is a multidimensional volume determined by several climatic variables. Think of the climate envelope as Goldilocks' preferences but for many environmental variables. Just outside the envelope, coffee plants are stressed, may never set fruit, and are more susceptible to pests. Further outside the climate envelope, the conditions exceed the physiological tolerance of coffee and the plants succumb. For coffee plants, the "just right" is largely determined by annual rainfall and minimal temperatures (Ferreira et al. 2019).

Rainfall largely determines how much water, essential for photosynthesis, is available to the plant. The ideal rainfall for Arabica is 1,400– 2,000 mm and 2,000–2,500 mm for Robusta. It is not just total rainfall that matters; the seasonality of rainfall can affect plants, including coffee. The rainy season in Costa Rica is from May through November. Coffee flowers at the end of the dry season, during April and May, and the wet season is when the fruits develop.

Temperature, like water, strongly affects the biochemistry of plants by determining the rate of biochemical reactions as well as transpiration, the loss of water through the leaves. If it's too cold, ice crystals harm plant cells unless they have particular adaptations, and if it's too hot, essential proteins start to change their shape and too much water is lost through the leaves. Most enzymes, proteins that speed up biochemical reactions, typically have a narrow range where they are optimally efficient. The optimal temperatures for Arabica are 22°C during the day and 18°C at night (Descroix and Snoeck

2012). This is important because, with daytime temperatures that exceed 25°C, plants will see reduced photosynthesis, reduced fruit set, and increased disease, all of which are a big problem for coffee production. Coffee plants are also sensitive to temperature fluctuations in the short-term. Coffee can physiologically adapt to changing temperatures after several weeks, but daily temperature fluctuations can stress Arabica coffee.

Within the native range of extant coffee species, the optimal conditions for coffee are found in the tropics, and most species of coffee are found specifically in the moist evergreen rainforest in Africa, Madagascar, the Arabian Peninsula, and Southeast Asia. In the Western Hemisphere, coffee is grown from Brazil north to Mexico and on numerous islands where higher elevations are available. In Central and South America, Arabica dominates the coffee market and is mostly found on the slopes of mountains between the lowland rainforest and montane forest. The exception is Brazil, where coffee is grown in the southeastern portion of the country that is typically lower in elevation and on more level terrain (Harvey et al. 2021). These conditions are also found, unsurprisingly, in the mid-elevational regions of Costa Rica. Most Arabica plantations are in the elevational band between the montane forest and the lowland tropical rainforest, which is more appropriate for Robusta and other species of coffee. Since Costa Rica primarily grows Arabica (currently), the impacts of the coffee industry are largely limited to mid-elevational tropical rainforests. Where there is appropriate rainfall and temperature, different coffee species can be found from sea level up to 2500 m (~8200 ft). Most species occur in relatively narrow elevation bands, but several including *C. eugenioides*, *C. canephora*, and *C. liberica*, have relatively broad elevational requirements (Ferreira et al. 2019, 6).

While Arabica is considered a higher quality coffee than Robusta, the difference in the growing conditions for each means that many coffee farmers around the world prefer to grow Robusta, since it is generally more tolerant, easier to grow, produces more coffee cherries, and its coffee beans contain more caffeine. While very few coffee-growing countries around the world produce more Robusta than Arabica, with the notable exception of Vietnam, many countries produce at both ends of the quality spectrum with high-quality Arabica varietals for the luxury market and a large amount of Robusta destined to be sold on the bottom shelf of the grocery store.

Within Costa Rica, there are eight coffee-growing regions. The names of the regions are based on the subtleties of coffee flavor that are thought to be the consequence of small differences in climate and soils between the different regions. Moving along the highlands in the northwest to the southeast, the regions are Guanacaste, Valle Occidental, Valle Central, Tres Rios, Tarrazu, Turrialba, Orosi, and Blanca. Variation in climate in Costa Rica derives from the variation in elevation interacting with major air currents. The predominant winds move moist warm air from the Atlantic to the northern half of Costa Rica. When this moisture-laden air is pushed up by the central highlands, it cools and loses the capacity to hold on to the moisture, so it rains over the eastern regions. The western side of Costa Rica experiences a rain shadow—a deficit of precipitation. Only in the highlands of the western region is there regular rainfall.

Precipitation and temperature are the primary drivers of the distributions of most plants—not just coffee. These two factors determines where the major biomes (e.g., desert, grasslands, moist tropical forest) are found. Other types of forests and habitats within the tropics include seasonal tropical forests, such as those found in the Guanacaste region in northwest Costa Rica. Seasonal tropical forests have a long and hot dry period that most coffee varieties cannot tolerate. Crops found in the tropical seasonal forests of Costa Rica are rice, sugar cane, and, to a lesser extent, oil palm. It may seem contradictory that rice is so important in such a dry region, but rice fields exist where large amounts of irrigation are possible (https://ipad.fas.usda.gov/highlights/2017/09/ca/index.htm). Ranching is also expansive in Guanacaste and pervades the culture there. Climate change threatens the dry tropical forests and crops, as the Guanacaste region is experiencing longer drought periods (Stan et al. 2020).

On the opposite end from the dry region is the high montane forest and paramo. At very high elevations, the year-round temperatures are too cool for coffee, and paramo vegetation is above the tree line. In the Americas, paramo and high montane forests can be found along the Andes. In Costa Rica, paramo is found in a small narrow strip in the highest parts of Cordillera Talamanca. Tropical montane forests, often called cloud forests, are situated between lowland forests and paramo. There, the trees are evergreen, but the canopy can often be shorter. Tropical montane forests are popular tourist destinations because orchids and other epiphytes, which are normally out of sight high in the canopy, are now within arm's reach. Moreover, the hummingbirds that are associated with these plants are also more visible. Paramo occurs above the tree line, where only shrubs, grasses, and other forbs grow. No commercial crops are grown in the paramo, although small ranching operations can be found in some areas.Given that montane forests and paramo are likely to warm in the future, coffee will likely be able to be grown in these regions. Paramo and tropical mountain forests are already endangered with many endemic species, so climate change is a particularly dangerous threat (Mata-Guel 2023). Endemic species are organisms that have a limited distribution and, in Costa Rica, many endemic species occur within a narrow elevational band. Much of the paramo is protected in Costa Rica, but that will not stop these areas from transforming and losing the many unique species that live there.

Tropical rainforests grow in the northeast quadrant and the southern half of Costa Rica. Tropical rainforests have high, dense canopies, epiphytes growing on the upper branches, and lianas (woody vines) growing down from the treetops to reach the forest floor below. New World (Neotropic) rainforests are among the most biologically diverse habitats in the world. In these areas, bananas and pineapples are grown and, to a lesser extent, beans, sugar cane, and other crops (https://www.fao.org/3/Y4632E/y4632e0a.htm#fn29). Ranching also occurs in areas that would otherwise be rainforest. Taken together, ranching, for beef and dairy, is the expansive land use in Costa Rica (https://www.fao.org/3/Y4632E/y4632e0a.htm#fn29).

CLIMATE CHANGE AND COFFEE

One of the issues that coffee farmers now face is a rapidly changing climate that is altering precipitation, temperature, as well as variability in both those factors. Markets and climate change are the primary forces that drive the global expansion of coffee into new regions or the abandonment of plantations (Ambinakudige and Choi 2009, Chaves et al. 2020, Harvey et al. 2021). Coffee plantations are expected to move up in elevation with increasing temperatures and changes in precipitation regimes (Harvey et al. 2021). In addition, the increasing temperatures caused by climate change and resistance to leaf rust may also be driving the expansion of the production of Robusta coffee. The need for Arabica alternatives has led Costa Rica, along with Nicaragua, to lift the ban on Robusta production. In other cases, governments are actively promoting the expansion of Robusta into lowlands and increasing deforestation or replacing Arabica plantations (Harvey et al. 2021). In some areas, coffee plantations are being abandoned, as the pressures of climate change and the difficulties of market volatility have made coffee farming more difficult as well as less profitable. This does not mean they are being converted back to forest. In most cases, these cleared areas are being replanted with other crops (Harvey et al. 2021). In Costa Rica, abandoned plantations are often converted to sugarcane and other crops (Harvey et al. 2021).

Several studies predict that worldwide coffee production will decline in light of climate change (Grüter et al. 2022) by up to 50 percent (Ovalle-Rivera et al. 2015) and affect 100 million workers by 2050 (Bunn et al. 2015). To a much lesser extent, coffee production can expand in some regions. One area where there can be considerable expansion of coffee in response to climate change is Ethiopia, where there could be a fourfold increase in land suitable for coffee (Moat et al. 2017). Imbach and colleagues (2017) predict a more dire situation for Central and South America—a reduction of 73 percent and 88 percent in coffee suitable areas under mid- and high-warming scenarios, respectively. With increasing temperatures, appropriate coffee areas move upslope. Areas with reduced mountain areas for future coffee regions include Nicaragua, Honduras, and Venezuela, and areas with expanded areas for future coffee growing include Mexico, Guatemala, Colombia, and Costa Rica. However, many of these areas where coffee can grow are currently forested and will present a conflict between coffee cultivation and forest conservation.

Evolutionary adaptation to climate change is one mitigating factor that can ameliorate the loss of area in future warming models. Incorporating adaptation into climate change models requires knowing the genes and gene interactions that are associated with coffee physiology. However, adaptation to abiotic factors, in this case, water availability and temperature, does not necessarily affect how plants respond to biotic factors, such as pests. A review by Pham and colleagues (2019) suggests that the effects of climate change will likely be negative, with small positive effects of increased pollination and carbon dioxide concentrations.

Climate change may force some farmers and governments to reconsider the use of *C. canephora*, which is generally more tolerant of higher temperatures and grows at lower elevations. However, even *C. canephora* has physiological limits, and expected temperature increases stress *C. canephora* (Kath et al. 2020). Tournebize and colleagues (2022) examined several genes of wild *C. canephora* across the range from herbarium specimens and found that this species would have reduced cultivation areas in Africa.

Complicating changes in distribution and abundance associated with climate change is the fact that organisms are often dependent on many other species, which may also be sensitive to climate conditions in very different ways. Computational models by Imbach and colleagues (2017) predict a loss of pollinators over much of the coffee-growing regions, with much smaller areas increasing in pollinator diversity. Increasing temperatures are expected to benefit the coffee borer beetle (Jaramillo et al. 2011). Therefore, the net effect of climate change on coffee plants and their associated species is incredibly difficult to predict.

KNOWN UNKNOWNS: INVASIVE SPECIES

Invasive species impact nearly every dimension of our lives, and we spend tens of billions of dollars to battle invasive species that have already been established (Bradshaw et al. 2016). Invasive insects serve as vectors for disease spread, such as the Asian tiger mosquito, which is a carrier of West Nile virus—a disease that impacts both humans and birds (Goldberg, Anderson, and Hamer 2010). Invasive species threaten food security in both production and storage. Coffee is impacted by several invasive species, with the coffee borer beetle in the Americas being a prime example, and the outlook looks grim for controlling the spread of new insects (Venette and Hutchison 2021). Using natural enemies of insect pests has yielded mixed results (Garcia et al. 2020). In addition to treating internationally traded goods, monitoring fields and farmer training will go a long way in managing invasive species. There are a number of coffee pests in Africa, which can potentially affect coffee crops in Latin America. Will these species arrive on the shores of Costa Rica? Their arrival seems inevitable, but the exact timing remains beyond our ability to predict. There is also the possibility of existing Costa Rican species evolving the ability to be pests of coffee. Since evolvability includes random mutations, the ability to predict such changes is beyond our grasp. The combination of the extent of coffee farming in Costa Rica, the density of plants, and the importance of coffee to Costa Ricans makes for a worrisome situation in which a new pest could be particularly devastating to coffee growing. At the moment, vigilance and prevention of new invasive species are the best pathways.

GENETIC MODIFICATION AND COFFEE

Biologists now have powerful tools at their disposal to alter the genome of coffee plants to increase efficiencies or to increase disease resistance. One approach to genetic modification is to immerse plants in a solution containing the bacterium *Agrobacterium tumefaciens.* This naturally occurring bacterium infects plants and causes them to grow tumors by inserting its genes into the plant's genome. *Agrobacterium* can be modified to contain a gene of interest, and the bacterium will insert the new gene into the plant gene. This technique has been used extensively in agriculture and research to create plants with desired traits or to study plant genomes (Clough and Bent 1998). Leroy and colleagues (2000) used *Agrobacterium* to insert the *cry1Ac* gene of *Bacillus thuringiensis* (Bt) into *C. canephora* and *C. arabica*. The *cry1Ac* gene produces a protein that is toxic to many herbivorous insects and is used to control pests in crops or even broadcast to control pests in the wild, such as spongy moths (*Lymantria dispar*) in the northeastern United States, where they are not native. When inserted into coffee plants, the *cryA1c* gene produces the insecticidal protein and is able to resist the coffee leaf miner (*Perileucoptera coffeella*). Much more research needs to be done so these technologies can be scaled up for coffee, but Bt is already used in most corn and other crops. One criticism of using genetically modified crops is the potential for the gene to enter the population of a nontarget species through hybridization. The issue then would be that a wild plant would produce a protein and negatively affect native and potentially beneficial insects that forage on the plant. However, since there are no plants in the genus *Coffea,* other than cultivated species, there is no chance that genes will enter the population of wild plants. There is also evidence that there is little hybridization between cultivated and wild *Coffea* species, so Bt coffee could potentially be used in Africa but more research should be done on the movement of genes between *Coffea* species. If Bt can be successfully grown at a commercial scale, it could potentially reduce the need for chemical pesticides in the environment as well as exposure of pesticides to coffee workers.

Another new tool for altering genomes is the CRISPR-Cas9 (CRISPR) approach, which was derived from a pathway in bacteria that breaks up viral genomes. CRISPR can be used to alter genomes in plants and animals. Like *Agrobacterium,* CRISPR can be used to deliver desired genes to more precise locations in the genome than Agrobacterium; it can be used in single cells, tissues, or whole organisms (Barrangou and Doudna 2016). Because gene insertion is so precise, CRISPR can be used to turn other genes off and on as well as for genes that produce a desired protein. CRISPR can be used in conjunction with *Agrobacterium* to introduce genes to targets in whole organisms. For example, Leibrock et al. (2022) and colleagues identified targets in the coffee genome where CRISPR could turn off the genes that produce caffeine. Breitler and colleagues (2018) examined the genome of *C. canephora* and found a multitude of targets for molecular editing that would alter coffee in many ways. However, signaling pathways in organisms are notoriously complex, and it will be a number of years before the full potential of genome editing can be realized. But, theoretically, coffee could be manipulated to mitigate the environmental effects associated with climate change and pests. For the consumer, genetic engineering can open up a whole new world of coffee flavors.

COFFEE CONSERVATION

Currently, we do not have the ability to alter genomes without an existing template. For example, we can move genes with desired traits from one organism to another. However, creating completely novel genes with desired effects is quite another thing. Therefore, scientists need existing species as a source of genes. Transitioning genes from one organism to another is more likely to work when species are more related to each other. For coffee, this means the over one hundred and twenty species that are not sold commercially may hold genes that are potentially useful for fighting pests and adapting to climate change. Knowing what diversity we have and conserving populations should be of concern for those who love coffee and coffee culture.

Herbaria are collections of plant material that allow us to inventory what species are known. Typically, herbarium specimens constitute pressed and dried leaves and, ideally, flowers and fruit. Important information that goes along with a specimen includes location information (the more precise, the better), collector information, date, and often other species that are growing with the specimen are noted. Herbarium specimens are documented occurrences and can be used to understand the distribution of a plant and how distributions change over time. Modern herbaria may also preserve leaves and seeds in a deep freeze to make nucleic acids (DNA and RNA) available for study. Under proper conditions, plant specimens can last well over a hundred years. The greatest threat to a plant collection is neglect, but also mold, insects, fire, and mishandling brittle specimens.

Herbaria may also contain coffee species unknown to science. Expeditions may be conducted by specialists in particular taxonomic groups in remote areas. Under these conditions, botanists will collect as many specimens as they can in the hopes that another specialist can examine specimens outside their own area of expertise. *Coffea* specimens are found in herbaria throughout the world, and expeditions are still seeking *Coffea* specimens (Charrier et al. 2012). There are, very likely, undescribed species of coffee existing in herbaria, just waiting for the right set of eyes (or DNA to be extracted). A database to explore Coffea species in collections is available at http://publish.plantnet-project.org/project/wildcofdb. Publicly available data such as these should facilitate and speed up communication between biologists in the field and laboratories.

Living collections can be found in arboretums or *in situ* collections (Charrier et al. 2012). The *in situ* collections would have native plants growing on their properties, whereas many living collections, like arboreta, have non-native plants growing on the property. Living collections are important because seeds cannot withstand dehydration. One drawback of living collections is that the growing conditions are the same as the conditions for cultivation. Another drawback of living collections is the cost of maintaining plants as well as the risk of catastrophic conditions such as hurricanes and landslides. One coffee worth pursuing in living collections is *C. rhombifolia*, a species found in drier regions. Unfortunately, no living specimens are available, and the species is currently found in politically unstable regions (Charr et al. 2020). This species could lead to commercial coffee plants that are more tolerant of drought. On the opposite end of the spectrum, *C. congensis* is adapted to wetlands (Charr et al. 2020).

Cryopreservation is the freezing of plant embryos or pollen for long-term storage and is not commonly used for coffee plants (Charrier et al. 2012).

This is particularly true for *C. canephora*, which has a less predictable genetic makeup as a result of cross-pollination (Zamarripa and Pétiard 2004). Although living plants can be revived from frozen tissue, cryopreservation is costly and energy-intensive (Walters and Pence 2021). In situ conservation of wild coffee species can be accomplished by setting aside of natural areas that contain *Coffea* species—known and unknown. This is not to say that humans should be excluded from these areas, but forest management practices in areas that harbor *Coffea* species should seek to conserve viable populations.

In addition to climate change and invasive pests, urbanization is a threat to the future of coffee farming. Harvey and colleagues (2021) report on the loss of land appropriate for coffee farming due to urbanization. Other agricultural land uses can, and often are, converted to coffee growing. The primary reason that urbanization is a threat to coffee growing is that, once areas become urbanized, the change is permanent.

Chapter 5

Coffee in Contemporary Costa Rica

THE LEGACIES OF COFFEE PRODUCTION IN LATIN AMERICA

In the coffee-growing countries of Latin America, the political economy of coffee is central to understanding the modern-day economic, social, and political systems of coffee-producing countries. One of the most important legacies of Spanish colonialism was the initiation of a labor system based on the use of force and the way that has percolated throughout Latin America to this day. From the earliest days of the colonial period, the Spaniards saw the people of Latin America as a labor force to be utilized in enterprises that would enrich the Spanish economy, with little regard to much else. The use of indigenous forced labor and then slave labor contributed to the formation of a colonial oligarchy that governed the region for decades and, in many important ways, still does.

Another important legacy of Spanish colonialism is the stark social stratification throughout most of the region. The high levels of social stratification can be seen throughout the region, and there are a number of striking examples of social stratification and income inequality. Among coffee-growing countries, El Salvador stands out as one of the most important examples of both. Throughout much of its history, El Salvador was governed by an oligarchy made up of coffee barons known as the fourteen families who were said to control the vast majority of the land of El Salvador. The dominance of the coffee elite was solidified during the nineteenth-century national period in which the colonial elite merged with recent European immigrants to create family coffee dynasties. "These coffee dynasties are cognatic descent groups that trace their lineage through both males and females to a founding male ancestor, usually the nineteenth-century immigrant of a colonial aristocrat who founded the family coffee enterprise" (Paige 1997, 16).

The story of the fourteen families is important to the understanding of the role of coffee in the nineteenth and twentieth centuries and the consequences of the labor relations that dominated El Salvador during that time. While books about El Salvador are replete with mentions of the fourteen families, there is really no definition of who they are or which specific families are included. The point of the story of the fourteen families is to illustrate just how dominant many of the elites were in nineteenth and twentieth-century Central America. As such, the fourteen families tended to own the most productive agricultural land for coffee, but also for cotton and sugar. These holdings meant that by the early 1980s, they received about 75 percent of the total export earnings of the country because about 2 percent of the population controlled around 60 percent of the arable land. The land concentration in El Salvador is further illustrated by the fact that only 5 percent of the 400,000 families engaged in agriculture did so on plots of 10 hectares or more. In fact, in 1980, 60 percent of the rural population had no land at all (Beverley 1982, 55).

This sort of dominance of the coffee elite over land and labor helped create economic systems that were heavily reliant on coffee exports to the exclusion of other parts of the economy. This reliance on coffee exports also meant that the coffee elite was extremely intolerant of even the smallest amount of dissent, and almost all the political regimes of Latin America gave a lot of power to the chief executive to squelch any and all dissent. For much of the twentieth century, the use of violence, particularly in Central America, was a key feature of the relationship between the coffee elite and workers.

In recent years, however, the power of the traditional oligarchy has receded somewhat and has been replaced by a new type of left-wing populist politician who now uses social stratification as a political tool to win votes by promising economic change to the poorest segments of society. Blanco and Grier (2011) found that electing a president from a leftist political party in Latin America hinges on two main factors. The first factor is natural resource abundance, including agricultural products, and the second is past political discrimination and government crises. They also found that countries that were more open to international trade were less likely to elect a leftist president (25). It also appears that much of the current wave of leftist victories in Latin America over the last decade or so is the product of a strong anti-incumbent wave that has its roots in the persistent poverty and lack of solutions from any part of the political spectrum, which is often highly corrupt. The real question is whether left-wing populism in the region represents a long-term preference of the electorate or a passing political moment. The data on coffee production, inequality, and average income show that many coffee-producing countries still struggle with inequality and low incomes (table 5.1).

Due to the manner in which the coffee industry developed in many parts of Latin America, there is a great deal of poverty and inequality in many countries that produce coffee, and these problems have proved difficult to solve. While Costa Rica, like any country, is not perfect, it has been able to build a consensus on the basic parameters of government and the manner in which it interacts with the people, something that is often elusive elsewhere. Much of this progress, however, has been difficult to maintain as the 2008–2009 global recession significantly impacted the Costa Rican economy, followed a little more than a decade later by COVID-19.

The biggest issue with both the 2008–2009 global recession and the pandemic is that they greatly impacted the tourism industry, which consequently affected most other sectors of the economy. These economic downturns put a sharp focus on what many Costa Ricans see as the modern failings of the political system. These problems have tended to manifest themselves in lowered participation in the political system and a growing dissatisfaction with democracy. For instance, "large majorities of Costa Ricans do not identify with any party, and only a quarter say they are satisfied with democracy. Outgoing president Carlos Alvarado will leave with one of the lowest approval ratings in the Americas, after a lackluster four years in office marked by corruption scandals" (Carnegie Endowment for International Peace 2022).

The combination of these crises has created a mountain of problems that have been difficult for the government to fix, and the political system has been under a great deal of strain over the last couple of decades. In addition, Costa Ricans have become increasingly dismayed by the growth of government and the increasingly high levels of corruption. The diffuse nature of the political party system can be seen in the election in 2022 for president, which requires

Table 5.1 Data on Coffee Production, Inequality, and Average Income

Country	*2020 Coffee Production in 60-KG Bags*	*Gini Index*	*Average Income in USD*
Brazil	63,400,000	48.3	7,629
Colombia	14,300,000	54	5,246
Honduras	6,100,000	48.2	2,236
Mexico	4,000,000	45.2	7,750
Peru	3,794,000	43.8	5,956
Guatemala	3,750,000	48.3	3,930
Nicaragua	2,650,000	46.2	1,719
Costa Rica	1,450,000	49.3	10,792
El Salvador	600,000	38.8	3,398
Ecuador	497,000	47.3	4,696

Source: Data collected from the International Coffee Organization and from World Bank.

a candidate to receive 40 percent of the vote to avoid a runoff election. The Costa Rican political party system has become so fragmented that there were an incredible twenty-five candidates for the first round, which produced an electoral matchup between a candidate who had never been elected to office (Ricardo Chaves Robles) and another who was a former president and the son of Costa Rican political legend Jose Figueres (José María Figueres).

> Many Costa Ricans regarded the runoff as a choice between two highly imperfect candidates. Chaves, who projected himself as an anti-politics maverick and whose second-place finish in the first round had been largely unexpected, was demoted at the World Bank due to sexual harassment of junior staffers and then faced a campaign financing scandal. Figueres was unable to shake off accusations of large-scale corruption during his first presidency from 1994 to 1998. (Carnegie Endowment for International Peace 2022)

Like many citizens in mature democracies, many Costa Ricans are self-critical of their democratic system and hold negative views of the status of Costa Rican democracy. This is not a new phenomenon, as Seligson and Booth (1993) found that opinions regarding democracy were weaker in Costa Rica than in Nicaragua, which was emerging from the Somoza era and the civil war that ended it. That said, it appears that the Costa Rican critique of its political system has become more pronounced as the World Justice Project (2022, 6) found that despite improvement in some areas, Costa Ricans have "deteriorating perceptions of government accountability and worsening perceptions of corruption. At the regional level, prominent trends include deteriorating perceptions of fundamental freedoms, low levels of trust in institutions, and weakened confidence in criminal justice system performance."

In addition to the political and economic impacts of the COVID-19 pandemic, it also served to change some of the labor migration patterns among those who labor in the coffee fields. Throughout much of the Latin American coffee industry, there is reliance on migrant labor to harvest their crops, which are often low-paid workers working long hours and being paid piecemeal for each basketful of harvested ripe coffee cherries. In Costa Rica, these migrants include workers coming from other parts of the country to the coffee-growing region to work during the four-month harvest season and others who work outside their home country on a seasonal basis. Costa Rica is a particularly stark example of the need for migrant labor as the country relies heavily on such workers. For instance, in 2020 at the height of the COVID-19 pandemic, officials from Costa Rica's National Institute of Coffee (ICAFE) worried that they would not be able to find enough workers to harvest that year's coffee crop. ICAFE estimated that the Costa Rican coffee industry would need approximately 74,000 coffee workers, putting the harvest particularly at risk that year (Murillo 2020).

THE FUTURE OF COSTA RICAN COFFEE

Since the end of the Costa Rican civil war, many coffee farmers, from large-scale to very small-scale producers, feel that their place in the political, social, and economic life of the country is under attack. This attitude began in the post-civil war era, during which a number of social and tax reforms that would ultimately diminish the power of the coffee growers were being debated and has more or less been present ever since. Not surprisingly, there was a lot of angst among the coffee farmers and their supporters, who often used stark language regarding the role of coffee in Costa Rica's future. For instance, a 1951 editorial written for the Costa Rican newspaper *La Nacion*, while the government was debating a number of measures that would strongly affect the coffee industry, declared the following: "Those coffee growers must not disappear, even if death threatens them as a result of the tendency to overburden them with taxes. They must not disappear because this fortunate distribution of land in small plots has endowed our country with a consistency of order, a spirit of peace, a love of freedom and a solid foundation for democracy" (Winson 1984, 38).

Usually referred to as the rural democracy thesis, the idea that Costa Rican democracy and its long-term stability were created and encouraged by the humble, hardworking, family-oriented coffee farmer on his own small plot is one of the most important stories of Costa Rican nationalism. Costa Rican scholar John Booth argues that a close examination of Costa Rican history reveals that some but not all of the rural democracy thesis is substantiated since, "Costa Rica's isolation, emergent racial homogeneity, and poverty bred relative economic equality, a tradition of and taste for civilian rule, weak military institutions and egalitarian social values." (50) Many tourists, as well as some scholars, will often paint an overly rosy picture of Costa Rica as an idyllic paradise, particularly juxtaposed to its neighbors. While the country is, of course, not perfect, there are many factors in Costa Rican history that differentiate it from its neighbors and make it a politically and socially unique place. A good measure of this uniqueness comes from Costa Rica's dedication to the coffee industry and the historical process in which the coffee industry was able to foster a modicum of social and economic equality in a region in which any level of equality is rare.

Even if the rural democracy thesis is not an entirely accurate portrait of Costa Rican political, economic, and social development, its basic parameters are a great source of pride for many Costa Ricans. The fact of the matter is that many Costa Ricans, especially coffee farmers, believe in the notion that their lifestyle is central to any understanding of Costa Rica and that it was people like them who built the foundation of a modern and peaceful Costa Rica. When traveling in rural Costa Rica, you will hear again and again the idea that Costa Rica is a coffee country, and many Costa Ricans will gladly tell stories about the multi-generational hard work that it took to build a coffee farm. To many people in coffee-growing regions like Tarrazú or Dota in the Los Santos region, coffee farming is central to what it means to be Costa Rican. Because of this, it is important to conceptualize coffee farming as more than just a vocation and source of income, but a lifestyle. Since its beginnings in the late eighteenth century, but particularly since the end of the Costa Rican civil war, the coffee industry has experienced many ups and downs, particularly with regard to the price they receive for their coffee. For most coffee farmers, they cannot conceive of living any other way than with the rhythm of the coffee fields. As such, they understand that there will be fluctuations in price and that there will be both good years as well as bad years. Samper (2010, 75) puts it this way:

> From their own experience and that of their parents or grandparents, Costa Rican coffee farmers learned to accept market crises as a fact of life and came to expect that sooner or later prices would recover. Few were willing to shift away from the crop that had been the mainstay of household incomes and had provided a degree of prosperity, despite the occasional bad years, for generations. Their attitude, rather, was usually to weather the storm and take certain steps to minimize losses during market downturns and to benefit from the subsequent recovery of world prices.

There is an interesting anecdotal way to know which years have had the most successful coffee harvests. If you see the same make and model of farm truck driven by multiple farmers, it is likely that whatever year the vehicle was produced was a good year for coffee as they used the extra money to upgrade their equipment. Coffee farmers know there will be ups and downs, and they prepare for them. Given the ups and downs of the coffee market and the inherent difficulties in ensuring that they can extract a living from growing coffee, many farmers have developed various strategies to increase their incomes. These include strategies to differentiate their coffee from other products on the international market by positioning their coffee for the luxury market. In addition, coffee farmers have also been able to adjust to the rigors of the modern coffee market by organizing themselves in two main ways: the *beneficio* (sometimes *micro beneficio* if it is very small) and the much larger coffee cooperative. Each of these arrangements seeks to maximize t amount of money that coffee producers can get for their crop, as each targe a slightly different export market. Additionally, some coffee growers in Costa Rica use some sort of outside certification to boost their income, such as bird friendly, organic and most often Fair Trade certification. For the most part, these certifications are used by coffee growers as supplemental rather than primary income. This is because normally, Costa Rican coffee growers will not even accept market price for their coffee due to its quality.

COSTA RICAN FARMERS TRY TO BOOST THEIR INCOMES IN NEW WAYS

Apart from the more formal strategies to boost incomes via the production of luxury or niche coffee through various certifications, many Costa Rican farmers engage in other strategies to boost income, such as planting other crops like plantains, bananas, or mangoes in their coffee fields. These are usually for family consumption and provide the added benefit of also providing shade for the coffee plants, as shade-grown coffee is typically considered higher quality. Another way in which many Costa Rican farmers tried to pivot away from the cultivation of coffee was by turning to cattle ranching. One of the chief attractions of moving from coffee cultivation to cattle ranching was that tending to pasture land for grazing is far less work than working a coffee plantation. For instance, "pasture in Costa Rica requires only 6 working days per hectare per year, compared with 37 for beans, 60 for rice, and 130 for coffee" (Carrière 1991, 17–18). A final strategy that some coffee farmers use is to either migrate to the United States temporarily if coffee prices are down or to get another job in Costa Rica. When we take students to Costa Rica, it seems like every Costa Rican we talk to has a coffee farm that we can visit in addition to their full-time job.

One of the more innovative ways that Costa Rican coffee farmers have tried to boost their income is by taking a page from the ecotourism industry and opening their farms and production facilities to tourist visits. These tours usually contain an educational element in which visitors are given information about different coffee varieties and processing methods, usually followed by a tour of the facility and, finally, a coffee cupping (the process of coffee tasting by which the quality of coffee for export is determined). Some of these tours even include a few minutes of picking coffee in the field. While some small farms and even a few cooperatives operate a coffee tour, the most famous of these tours is run by Costa Rican coffee giant Café Britt, which began its tours in 1991. While these coffee tours cost anywhere from $40 per person for the basic tour to $150 for a more involved tour (Café Britt), the income from these tours is actually a small fraction of the possible income from showing tourists the coffee plantation and processing facilities. The most promising part is the number of people who later buy coffee over the internet from producers like Café Britt because they have made a connection to the coffee during their visit. It is estimated that about 10 percent of those who go on a coffee tour on their Costa Rican vacation become regular customers of Café Britt's coffee through online purchasing (Pendergrast 2010).

Due to the popularity and reputation of Costa Rican coffee, there is a lot of growth potential for coffee tourism, as Costa Rica has the elements necessary for a successful coffee tourism business. These factors include a visit to a coffee-growing destination, the ability to experience a local coffee culture, and a place that is important in the history of coffee (Joliffe 2010). Obviously, the main coffee-growing regions in Costa Rica have each of these attributes, and the prospect for coffee tourism to become a large value-added enterprise is quite high. When you combine the quality of the coffee, the beauty of the landscape, and the friendliness of the people, the sky's the limit for Costa Rica coffee tourism.

COFFEE COOPERATIVE CASE STUDY: COOPETARRAZÚ IN SAN MARCOS DE TARRAZÚ

Due to the difficulties inherent in coffee cultivation, many farmers choose to contribute to a larger cooperative. The cooperative movement is a very important part of the Costa Rican economy across several types of products and services. "37% of the economically active population is directly or indirectly related to a cooperative. From the estimated 52,500 farmers growing coffee in Costa Rica, 26,881 are members of cooperatives" (Hopfensitz and Miquel-Florensa 2017, 627). While coffee is one of the most important sectors in the cooperative system, there are many agricultural cooperatives as well as cooperatives for utilities such as electricity.

One of the most interesting examples of a Costa Rican coffee cooperative is CoopeTarrazú, located south of the capital in the Los Santos area of Tarrazú. CoopeTarrazú was founded by 228 small coffee farmers in San Marcos de Tarrazú on October 13, 1960, with an initial investment of $5800 and the stated goals of producing high-quality coffee in a sustainable way that improves biodiversity (Monge 2010). Since that time, CoopeTarrazú has become the hub of San Marcos de Tarrazú and the surrounding area, providing myriad services for the community. The cooperative itself has a large coffee mill with a capacity of 150,000 fanegas (a fanega is a measurement equal to 1.58 U.S. bushels) and many collection points (*recibidores)* for coffee spread around the countryside. In addition to the technical services provided to farmers, CoopeTarrazú has several retail outlets around San Marcos, including gas stations, hardware stores, and supermarkets. While the retail outlets provide much-needed services for this very rural area, the power of the cooperative rests on two main pillars: technical assistance to boost yield and quality and the cooperative's bargaining power to get the highest price possible for their coffee.

The bargaining power of CoopeTarrazú is especially important because out of the 5,000 or so members, 66 percent produce 50 fanegas or less, and 83 percent produce 100 fanegas or less (Monge 2010). The bargaining power of CoopeTarrazú and its ability to bring together farmers to negotiate the price of coffee as a group is exactly why the Costa Rican government encouraged the cooperative movement starting after the Great Depression. Since CoopeTarrazú comprises many small and medium-sized operations, there are a number of strategies employed by both the cooperative and the individual farmers to hold down costs and increase income. One of the primary services provided by the cooperative is low-cost fertilizer that is produced in-house. The production of low-cost fertilizer for its members also serves an important environmental purpose as it is produced from the by-product of coffee production (expended coffee cherries) that is brought to the processing plant by its members. Additionally, the cooperative will often provide low-cost or no-cost technical assistance to members for the mediation of diseases, pests, and strategies to boost yield and the percentage of high-quality coffee beans suitable for export (Monge 2010). In fact, one of CoopeTarrazú's most recent successes is the increase in the amount of export-quality coffee produced by its farmers.

The process by which CoopeTarrazú collects, processes, and sells its coffee is highly regulated and follows procedures set by the National Coffee Institute (ICAFE) which was founded in 1933 to serve as the chief regulatory body for Costa Rican coffee. ICAFE also participates extensively in the research and development of coffee farming techniques to increase yields and quality and also develops coffee varietals for production. ICAFE takes an active role in the day-to-day operations of the coffee industry, including regulating the price paid to coffee farmers for their crop and the wages for the farm labor that collects it. The organization is funded by a 1.5 percent tax on coffee. Costa Rica, like many other coffee-growing countries in Latin America, has a unique measuring system for coffee known as the *cajuela*, a small box (*cajuela* comes from the Spanish word for box, caja) that holds approximately 12 kilograms of coffee. The Costa Rican Ministry of Labor sets the minimum price for coffee by the *cajuela,* which is currently $2 for the farm labor that collects the coffee. ICAFE provides the boxes to ensure they are a standard size.

After the farmer collects the coffee from the field and pays the coffee pickers for their work, the coffee is either taken to one of CoopeTarrazú's collection points or directly to the main facility in San Marcos de Tarrazú. Here, the farmer has his coffee measured out in another ICAFE-provided box (fanega). If it is later in the season (coffee picking season in Costa Rica is roughly November through March), the coffee is also monitored for the percentage of ripe red coffee cherries versus unripe green cherries. This is because, at the end of the harvest, the pickers will try to completely strip the plant of coffee cherries to ensure that they will grow back again in the subsequent growing season. Discerning the percentage of ripe cherries is done by taking a few random samples from the fanega and then removing the unripe green cherries, leaving only the ripe red ones. The percentage of red ripe coffee cherries in the batch dropped off at the cooperative is the percentage of the price they pay the farmer for the coffee; e.g., if the coffee is 70 percent red cherries, the farmer will receive 70 percent of the current market price. Once this process is completed, the farmer receives a voucher to be paid the following day. In order to monitor the amount of coffee picked and processed, the mill or cooperative must report the amount of coffee they have received to the government every 15 days.

The price of coffee that CoopeTarrazú pays to farmers is also highly regulated to ensure that the cooperative's profit does not exceed the legally mandated maximum of 12 percent. Coffee mills are legally required to post the current market price for coffee that they will pay. This is achieved by paying farmers in at least two stages. First, the farmer will receive the *adelanto* (advance), which is the minimum price that could be paid for the coffee. At the end of the season, a second payment is made, known as the *liquidacion* (settlement), which is the ICAFE-mandated price and is adjusted to ensure that the profit margin for the cooperative is no more than 12 percent. This final payment is determined by the larger coffee market and will sometimes be small or nonexistent if the price of coffee falls after the first payment, something that is certainly possible with a large harvest either in Costa Rica or worldwide.

Despite the many benefits of contributing to a coffee cooperative, some farmers choose to grow, process, and export their own coffee. These operations are referred to as a *microbeneficio* and use essentially the same processing machinery as a large cooperative, but on a much smaller scale. Often these operations specialize in producing luxury coffees, which is facilitated by having control over the entire coffee-growing process.

> The most dynamic sector at the retail end of the international coffee market has been the specialty coffee segment, which has grown in both absolute and relative terms while demand for regular kinds of coffee has stagnated or declined. The percentage of Costa Rican coffee sold in the specialty market has increased substantially since the early 1990s. Currently, most of this higher quality product is channeled through the Starbucks chain and the rest through wholesale

> brokers, some relatively small-scale roasters and retailers, or direct sales and mailing. (Samper 2003, 83)

Apart from the ability to (possibly) make more money in the luxury market, many farmers do not join a cooperative because they simply want to farm, process, and sell their coffee as they see fit without the need to follow the mandates of the cooperatives. This notion does not necessarily flow from the idea that they can make more money in the luxury market, but that they are fulfilling a long-held family tradition and want to do all the work themselves. In addition, despite many of the benefits of a cooperative, such as discounted supplies, there are often cooperative policies that push potential members away. Chief among them is receiving payment for their coffee over time rather than all of it at once. CoopeTarrazú started to see some of its members selling coffee in what is known as a side-sell or sometimes a farm-gate sale, which means that the coffee is sold to a onetime buyer without any sort of long-term contract and the farmer then receives all the money in a single payment, often more than the cooperative was offering. This is referred to as a farm-gate sale because the transaction occurs over the farm-gate via sellers that drive around the countryside looking for farmers willing to sell to them. This sort of behavior creates a problem for the cooperative as a member may consume the cooperative's services, then sell all or a portion of their coffee in a side-sell.

> Cooperativists face a real-world free-riding problem: Financial and technical assistance from the cooperative are guaranteed by membership independently of the production and hence of the contribution to the institution. Cooperative members therefore have the possibility to benefit from the "common services" while side-selling a part or all their high-quality harvest to the free market for higher prices. Side-selling is against cooperative rules, but punishment is very rare. (Hopfensitz and Miquel-Florensa 2017, 642)

Not surprisingly, this sort of behavior has led many members to question the efficacy of CoopeTarrazú's model. Ultimately, CoopeTarrazú boosted the initial payment to be more competitive with the short-term buyers and thus assumed more of the price risk of being the coffee (World Bank 2015, 80). This resulted in many farmers once again selling their coffee to the cooperative.

There are also cooperatives that suffer from bad or corrupt management and others that constantly have disputes between members and between members and the cooperative. CoopeTarrazú, in particular, suffered a major decline in competitiveness due to problems in the quality of the coffee they were producing, lack of funds, and lack of market access, all of which made membership in the cooperative much less attractive to potential members. In reaction to this, CoopeTarrazú's Board reworked its overall strategy and in 2003/2004 brought in all new management at a much higher cost (predominantly in higher salaries). The hiring of managers from outside of the organization goes against a long-held tradition in Costa Rican cooperatives of all types that managers should be hired from existing members (World Bank 2015, 8). Couple these issues with the difficulties in convincing a small-plot coffee farmer that the cooperative should hire an outside manager at a salary much larger than the farmer has ever made, and the cooperative found itself in a difficult position. However, once the benefits of professional management became apparent, such as better systems in the cooperative, a more streamlined payment, and most importantly, training that helped to mitigate disease and increased the percentage of the coffee harvest that was export quality, members became more comfortable with what the new managers were being paid.

MICROBENEFICIO CASE STUDY: BENEFICIO LA LÍA TARRAZÚ

Just down the road and up the mountain from CoopeTarrazú is Beneficio La Lía Tarrazú, an example of a small coffee operation outside of the larger cooperative system. Beneficio La Lía was founded in 2007 by two brothers, Luis Alberto and Oscar Monge Ureña, and was named after their mother, Doña Lia Ureña. Despite the fact that the *microbeneficio* is not as old as many in the region, the Monge family has farmed coffee in the region for generations. The Monge brothers have a number of small farms spread all over the region that contribute to the *beneficio* and specialize in the production of luxury coffee, such as gesha and bourbon varieties as well as honey process and a cinnamon process they developed themselves. Micro mills such as La Lia came to prominence in the last few decades as luxury coffee started to increase in popularity and the international market for them exploded. A big part of the reason that a farmer would have their own micromill rather than contribute to a larger cooperative is that with control over a larger part of the production process, they are better able to sell to the luxury market via very stringent quality control. For a cooperative such as CoopeTarrazú, they can collect high-quality coffee from the region and sell it above market price to large companies such as Starbucks or Green Mountain Coffee. La Lía, on the other hand, concentrates on having much more control over the process and thus receives an even higher price for their coffee. The Monge brothers' coffee has been very successful in international competitions, including winning first place in the Taza de la Excelencia in 2021 with a gesha coffee processed with the honey method. In order for operations such as La Lia to be successful it is necessary to both appeal to and integrate with the international market, particularly in Japan, as many of the very best Costa Rican coffees end up being consumed there.

The Monge brothers take advantage of providing value-added coffee to international consumers due to their various linkages to the international economy via a network of small coffee roasting firms in the United States, Europe, and Asia. One of the major advantages of being directly linked to the international economy is that they can demand prices that are considerably higher than the market price based on quality for the high-end coffee market. For instance, in the 2022 Cup of Excellence Costa Rica coffee auction, the top-scoring coffee in the auction received $140.10 per pound and the Monges, who scored the fifth-best coffee, received $61.50 a pound (Cup of Excellence 2022 Auction Results). This is for a year in which the average price of coffee on the New York Stock Exchange was approximately $2.14 per pound (Nasdaq Coffee Prices).

La Lia and other microbeneficios can produce high-quality coffee that fetches such high prices because they can control every aspect of the coffee production, from the way the plants are pruned and nurtured in the field to the manner in which they are processed after harvest. While the coffee produced by the large cooperatives is of very high-quality and is routinely sold above the stock exchange price, when coffee is contributed from hundreds of farmers in multiple locations, there is not a similar level of control over quality. In addition, microbeneficios such as La Lia can better upgrade and experiment with new techniques because the added income allows for better upgrading of techniques and equipment.

CONCLUSION

This book has examined the long-term evolution of coffee production in Costa Rica and the need for long-term economic success for the Costa Rican coffee industry and the manner in which it is enhanced and catalyzed by economic, social, political, and especially ecological sustainability. At the most basic level, it is necessary not just to preserve coffee farming as a viable long-term economic enterprise, but also to make sure that agricultural occupations generally are economically viable in the long-term. One thing that is encouraging about Costa Rica's approach to coffee production is the extent to which it is done by smallholders on family farms. One of the most important strategies for long-term profitability in coffee production is for these smallholder farms to take more of the profit from the supply chain via the adoption of value-added services to their coffee. While this can be seen in the luxury coffee market, coffee farmers in Costa Rica (and elsewhere) would be well served to do things like sell their coffee roasted on the international market directly. This is not a startling revelation; however, it will take concrete strategies for smallholder operations to better engage with the international market and capture more of the profit from the supply chain. Many of the strategies used in Costa Rica include the increase in microbeneficios, the focus on quality over quantity, and the increasing amount of coffee that is exported with value-added attributes such as roasted coffee.

Social and political sustainability flows directly from economic sustainability. If coffee is profitable in the long-term, it will increase the social stability of coffee by supporting farm families and the regions in Costa Rica that depend heavily on the production of coffee and while coffee is still an important cultural touchstone in Costa Rica, its economic importance has waned over time, and coffee producers do not hold the sort of power that they once did.

Ecological Sustainability

Functional ecosystems are essential for the long-term viability of the coffee industry. Soils that provide coffee nutrients depend on a rigorous network of fungi and beneficial bacteria that recycle nutrients from organic matter back to the coffee plant—replacing nutrients that are literally carted away to become the coffee in your cup. Some of this organic matter can be the unused parts of the coffee cherry, sparing nearby waterways where the waste was originally dumped, thereby closing the loop.

Birds, ants, and other predatory insects can help reduce the need for insecticides. By providing shade trees, farmers can not only provide important habitats for birds and other wildlife, but they can improve coffee flavor and demand a higher price for coffee. These win-win scenarios have other benefits. Increased avian diversity benefits other agricultural industries as well as the ecotourism industry. Shade trees also provide additional organic material for coffee plants, reduce pest plants, mitigate temperature fluctuations, and help hold soil. Shade trees and other nearby vegetation may also provide habitat for native bees and other pollinators, which increase coffee yields.

Some pests, like coffee rust, do not have any obvious biological control, so keeping this devastating fungus at bay requires careful observation by farmers and appropriate applications of fungicides. The future may hold novel treatments such as viruses that target pathogenic fungi. Another important pest is the coffee borer beetle. Research is currently underway to find parasitic wasps or other insects that can help reduce the population of borer beetles. Another approach to these issues is using genetically modified plants that are resistant to these pests. There are coffee varieties that are more resistant to coffee rust and the coffee borer beetle, but pathogens can evolve quickly. When society allows, technologies can help us stay ahead of pathogens.

The two forces that will shape the future of coffee are climate change and invasive species. Genetic modification will probably be necessary to create plants that persist in the weather regimes associated with climate change. But this will be tricky business. Ecology is complicated—particularly in the tropics, where most organisms are still unknown to science. Add new invasive species to the mix, and the future of coffee is even less certain. What we do know is that this crop is central to Costa Rica and its rich heritage, and coffee, in all of its delicious forms, is a shared joy in our world.

Despite the problems faced by many Costa Rican coffee producers, coffee will remain an important part of Costa Rican economics and culture for the foreseeable future. While this book examines the manner in which the importance of the Costa Rican coffee industry has declined over time, it should also be clear that the hardworking farmers of Costa Rica will continue to adapt to whatever situation confronts them and will continue to produce the best coffee in the world. In order to do this, it is necessary to find new ways to be both economically and ecologically sustainable through innovation because, for Costa Rican coffee farmers, producing coffee goes well beyond a job or even a livelihood; it is the manifestation of what it means to be Costa Rican.

Bibliography

Ambinakudige, S., and J. Choi. "Global coffee market influence on land-use and land-cover change in the Western Ghats Of India." *Land Degradation & Development* 20, no. 3 (2009): 327–335. https://doi.org/10.1002/ldr.921.

Ameringer, Charles D. *Democracy in Costa Rica.* New York: Praeger, 1982.

Anderson, Thomas P. *Matanza.* Willimantic: Curbstone Press, 1992.

Aranda, E., L. Duran, and E. Escamilla. "Vermicomposting in coffee cultivation." In *Coffee: Growing, Processing, Sustainable Production,* edited by J. N. Wintgens, 324–338. Verlag: Wiley-VCH, 2012.

Arce, Victor Julio Chavez, Raul Raudales, Rich Trubey, David I. King, Richard B. Chandler, and Carlin C. Chandler. "Measuring and managing the environmental cost of coffee production in Latin America." *Conservation and Society* 7, no. 2 (2009): 141–144.

Astorino, E. S. The great depression in Brazil. Dissertação de Mestrado, Faculdade de Economia, Administração e Contabilidade, Universidade de São Paulo, São Paulo, 2012. https://doi.org/10.11606/D.12.2012.tde-01022013-183158. Recuperado em 2022-07-05, de www.teses.usp.br.

Augelli, John P. "Costa Rica's frontier legacy." *Geographical Review* 77, no. 1 (January 1987): 1–16.

Bale, Rachael. "The disturbing secret behind the world's most expensive coffee." *National Geographic,* April 29, 2016. https://www.nationalgeographic.com/animals/article/160429-kopi-luwak-captive-civet-coffee-Indonesia, accessed January 14, 2023.

Bang, Christofer, Stanley H. Faeth, and John L. Sabo. "Control of arthropod abundance, richness, and composition in a heterogeneous desert city." *Ecological Monographs* 82, no. 1 (2012): 85–100.

Barrangou, Rodolphe, and Jennifer A. Doudna. "Applications of CRISPR technologies in research and beyond." *Nature Biotechnology* 34, no. 9 (2016): 933–941.

Bawin, Yves, Tom Ruttink, Ariane Staelens, Annelies Haegeman, Piet Stoffelen, Jean-Claude Ithe Mwanga Mwanga, Isabel Roldán-Ruiz, Olivier Honnay, and

Steven B. Janssens. "Phylogenomic analysis clarifies the evolutionary origin of Coffea arabica." *Journal of Systematics and Evolution* 59, no. 5 (2021): 953–963. https://doi.org/10.1111/jse.12694.

Bedoya-Durán, M. J., H. H. Jones, K. M. Malone, and L. C. Branch. "Continuous forest at higher elevation plays a key role in maintaining bird and mammal diversity across an Andean coffee-growing landscape." *Animal Conservation* 26, no. 5 (2023): 714–728. https://doi.org/10.1111/acv.12857.

Bell, John Patrick. *Crisis in Costa Rica: The 1948 Revolution.* Austin: University of Texas Press, 1971.

Beverley, John. "El Salvador." *Social Text* 5 (Spring 1982): 55–72.

Blanco, Luisa and Robin Grier. "Explaining the rise of left in Latin America." Pepperdine University, School of Public Policy Working Papers, 2011.

Booth, John. "Costa Rican Democracy." *World Affairs* 150, no. 1 (1987): 43–53.

Booth, John. *Costa Rica: Quest for Democracy.* Boulder: Westview, 1998.

Borrelli, Pasquale, Christine Alewell, Pablo Alvarez, Jamil Alexandre Ayach Anache, Jantiene Baartman, Cristiano Ballabio, Nejc Bezak, Marcella Biddoccu, Artemi Cerdà, Devraj Chalise, Songchao Chen, Walter Chen, Anna Maria De Girolamo, Gizaw Desta Gessesse, Detlef Deumlich, Nazzareno Diodato, Nikolaos Efthimiou, Gunay Erpul, Peter Fiener, Michele Freppaz, Francesco Gentile, Andreas Gericke, Nigussie Haregeweyn, Bifeng Hu, Amelie Jeanneau, Konstantinos Kaffas, Mahboobeh Kiani-Harchegani, Ivan Lizaga Villuendas, Changjia Li, Luigi Lombardo, Manuel López-Vicente, Manuel Esteban Lucas-Borja, Michael Märker, Francis Matthews, Chiyuan Miao, Matjaž Mikoš, Sirio Modugno, Markus Möller, Victoria Naipal, Mark Nearing, Stephen Owusu, Dinesh Panday, Edouard Patault, Cristian Valeriu Patriche, Laura Poggio, Raquel Portes, Laura Quijano, Mohammad Reza Rahdari, Mohammed Renima, Giovanni Francesco Ricci, Jesús Rodrigo-Comino, Sergio Saia, Aliakbar Nazari Samani, Calogero Schillaci, Vasileios Syrris, Hyuck Soo Kim, Diogo Noses Spinola, Paulo Tarso Oliveira, Hongfen Teng, Resham Thapa, Konstantinos Vantas, Diana Vieira, Jae E. Yang, Shuiqing Yin, Demetrio Antonio Zema, Guangju Zhao, and Panos Panagos. "Soil erosion modeling: A global review and statistical analysis." *Science of The Total Environment* 780 (2021): 146494. https://doi.org/10.1016/j.scitotenv.2021.146494.

Bradshaw, Corey J. A., B. Leroy, Céline Bellard, David Roiz, Céline Albert, Alice Fournier, Morgane Barbet-Massin, Jean-Michel Salles, Frédéric Simard, and Franck Courchamp. "Massive yet grossly underestimated global costs of invasive insects." *Nature Communications* 7 (2016): 12986.

Brando, C. H. J. "Harvesting and green coffee processing." In *Coffee: Growing, Processing, Sustainable Production*, edited by J. N. Wintgens, 610–721. Weinheim: Wiley-VCH. 2012.

Breitler, Jean-Christophe, Eveline Dechamp, Claudine Campa, Leonardo Augusto Zebral Rodrigues, Romain Guyot, Pierre Marraccini, and Hervé Etienne. "CRISPR/Cas9-mediated efficient targeted mutagenesis has the potential to accelerate the domestication of Coffea canephora." *Plant Cell, Tissue and Organ Culture (PCTOC)* 134, no. 39 (2016): 383–394. https://doi.org/10.1007/s11240-018-1429-2.

Brundtland, G. H. Our Common Future: Report of the World Commission on Environment and Development. Geneva, UN-Document A/42/427 (1987).

Bunn, Christian, Peter Läderach, Oriana Ovalle Rivera, and Dieter Kirschke. "A bitter cup: climate change profile of global production of Arabica and Robusta coffee." *Climatic Change* 129, no. 1 (2015): 89–101. https://doi.org/10.1007/s10584-014-1306-x.

Café Britt. https://www.coffeetour.com/, accessed February 6, 2023.

Carnegie Endowment for International Peace. "Costa Rica's New Populist President Could be a Lesson in Democracy–or a Worrying Trend." https://carnegieendowment.org/2022/05/.4/costa-rica-s-new-populist-president-could-be-lesson-in-democracy-or-worrying-trend-pub-87037, accessed June 19, 2023.

Carriere, Jean. "The crisis in Costa Rica: an ecological perspective." In *Environment and Development in Latin America*, edited by D. Goodman and M. Redclift, 184–204. CABI Databases, 1991.

Castillo, G., and J. N. Wintgens. "Nematodes in coffee." In *Coffee: Growing, Processing, Sustainable Production*, edited by J. N. Wintgens, 474–490. Weinheim: Wiley-VCH, 2012.

Castro-Tanzi, Sebastian, Thomas Dietsch, Natalia Urena, Lucia Vindas, and Mark Chandler. "Analysis of management and site factors to improve the sustainability of smallholder coffee production in Tarrazú, Costa Rica." *Agriculture, Ecosystems & Environment* 155 (2012): 172–181.

Caudill, S. Amanda, and Robert A. Rice. "Do bird friendly® coffee criteria benefit mammals? Assessment of mammal diversity in Chiapas, Mexico." *PLOS ONE* 11 (2016): e0165662. https://doi.org/10.1371/journal.pone.0165662.

Centeri, Csaba. 'Effects of grazing on water erosion, compaction and infiltration on grasslands." *Hydrology* 9, no. 2 (2022): 34.

Charr, Jean-Claude, Andrea Garavito, Christophe Guyeux, Dominique Crouzillat, Patrick Descombes, Coralie Fournier, Serigne N. Ly, Eva N. Raharimalala, Jean-Jacques Rakotomalala, Piet Stoffelen, Steven Janssens, Perla Hamon, and Romain Guyot. "Complex evolutionary history of coffees revealed by full plastid genomes and 28,800 nuclear SNP analyses, with particular emphasis on Coffea *canephora* (Robusta coffee)." *Molecular Phylogenetics and Evolution* 151 (2020): 106906. https://doi.org/10.1016/j.ympev.2020.106906.

Charrier, A., P. Lashermes, and A. B. Eskes. "Botany, genetics and genomics of coffee." In Coffee: Growing, Processing, Sustainable Production, edited by J.N. Wintgens, 25–60. Wiley-VCG, 2012.

Chasteen, John Charles. *Born in Blood & Fire: A Concise History of Latin America,* 4th Edition. New York: W.W. Norton, 2016.

Chaves, Leonardo Suveges Moreira, Jacob Fry, Arunima Malik, Arne Geschke, Maria Anice Mureb Sallum, and Manfred Lenzen. "Global consumption and international trade in deforestation-associated commodities could influence malaria risk." *Nature Communications* 11, no. 1 (2020): 1258. https://doi.org/10.1038/s41467-020-14954-1.

Church, George Earl. "Costa Rica." *The Geographical Journal* 10, no. 1 (July 1897): 56–84.

Clough, S. J., and A. F. Bent. "Floral dip: A simplified method for Agrobacterium-mediated transformation of Arabidopsis thaliana." *Plant Journal* 16, no. 6 (1998): 735–743. https://doi.org/10.1046/j.1365-313x.1998.00343.x.

Coffee Geography Magazine. https://coffeegeography.com/brazilian-coffee-regions/, accessed February 9, 2023.

Costanza, Robert, Ralph d'Arge, Rudolf De Groot, Stephen Farber, Monica Grasso, Bruce Hannon, Karin Limburg et al. "The value of the world's ecosystem services and natural capital." *Nature* 387, no. 6630 (1997): 253–260.

Cruz-Angón, A., and R. Greenberg. "Are epiphytes important for birds in coffee plantations? An experimental assessment." *Journal of Applied Ecology* 42, no. 1 (2005): 150–159. https://doi.org/10.1111/j.1365-2664.2004.00983.x.

Cruz-Angón, Andrea, Martha L. Baena, and Russell Greenberg. "The contribution of epiphytes to the abundance and species richness of canopy insects in a Mexican coffee plantation." *Journal of Tropical Ecology* 25, no. 5 (2005): 453–463. https://doi.org/10.1017/S0266467409990125.

Cruz, Consuelo. "Identity and Persuasion: How nations remember their pasts and make their futures." *World Politics* 52, no. 3 (2000): 275–312.

Constitución Politíca de la República de Costa Rica, November 7, 1949.

Cup of Excellence, 2021. "Costa Rica 2021." https://cupofexcellence.org/costa-rica-2021/, accessed February 2, 2023.

Cup of Excellence, 2022. "Costa Rica Coffee Auction Results." https://allianceforcoffeeexcellence.org/costa-rica-2022/#1626373223108-e0a94038-d157, accessed June 26, 2023.

Cup of Excellence, 2023. https://cupofexcellence.org/, accessed June 15, 2023.

Cure, José Ricardo, Daniel Rodríguez, Andrew Paul Gutierrez, and Luigi Ponti. "The coffee agroecosystem: bio-economic analysis of coffee berry borer control (*Hypothenemus hampei*)." *Scientific Reports* 10, no. 1 (2020): 12262. https://doi.org/10.1038/s41598-020-68989-x.

Daily Coffee News. "US State Department Confirms Withdrawal from the International Coffee Agreement," October 22, 2018, retrieved at https://dailycoffeenews.com/2018/10/22/us-state-department-confirms-withdrawal-from-the-international-coffee-agreement/#:~:text=The%20U.S.%20left%20the%20ICA,ICA%20under%20the%20George%20W, accessed June 6, 2022.

de la Fuente, Alejandro, and Ariela Gross. "Comparative studies of law, slavery and race in the Americas." *The Annual Review of Law and Social Science* 6 (2010): 469–485.

de León, Ana. "How Panamanian Coffee became an international luxury brand: Geisha Coffee." EFE News Service; Madrid, February 6, 2020. https://www.proquest.com/docview/2351570083?pq-origsite=summon&parentSessionId=WpEKcuCwnBENGW1e2lSEzfM6YFSfknZu1F0Hc%2F2xD%2FI%3D, accessed January 19, 2023.

De Pelsmacker, Patrick, Liesbeth Driesen, and Glenn Rayp. "Do consumers care about ethics? Willingness to pay for fair-trade coffee." *Journal of consumer affairs* 39, no. 2 (2005): 363–385.

Dell, Melissa. "The Persistent Effects of Peru's Mining Mita." *Econometrica* 78, no. 6 (2010): 1863–1903.

Denoeud, France, Lorenzo Carretero-Paulet, Alexis Dereeper, Gaëtan Droc, Romain Guyot, Marco Pietrella, Chunfang Zheng, Adriana Alberti, François Anthony, Giuseppe Aprea, Jean-Marc Aury, Pascal Bento, Maria Bernard, Stéphanie Bocs, Claudine Campa, Alberto Cenci, Marie-Christine Combes, Dominique Crouzillat, Corinne Da Silva, Loretta Daddiego, Fabien De Bellis, Stéphane Dussert, Olivier Garsmeur, Thomas Gayraud, Valentin Guignon, Katharina Jahn, Véronique Jamilloux, Thierry Joët, Karine Labadie, Tianying Lan, Julie Leclercq, Maud Lepelley, Thierry Leroy, Lei-Ting Li, Pablo Librado, Loredana Lopez, Adriana Muñoz, Benjamin Noel, Alberto Pallavicini, Gaetano Perrotta, Valérie Poncet, David Pot, Priyono, Michel Rigoreau, Mathieu Rouard, Julio Rozas, Christine Tranchant-Dubreuil, Robert VanBuren, Qiong Zhang, Alan C. Andrade, Xavier Argout, Benoît Bertrand, Alexandre de Kochko, Giorgio Graziosi, Robert J Henry, Jayarama, Ray Ming, Chifumi Nagai, Steve Rounsley, David Sankoff, Giovanni Giuliano, Victor A. Albert, Patrick Wincker, and Philippe Lashermes. "The coffee genome provides insight into the convergent evolution of caffeine biosynthesis." *Science* 345, no. 6201 (2014): 1181–1184. https://doi.org/10.1126/science.1255274.

Descroix, Frédéric, and J. Snoeck. "Environmental factors suitable for coffee cultivation." In *Coffee: Growing, Processing, Sustainable Production*, edited by J. N. Witgens, 168–181. Wiley-VCH, 2012

Dicum, Gregory. "Colony in a Cup." *Gastronomica* 3, no. 2 (2003): 71–77.

Dorcas, Michael E., and John D. Willson. "Innovative methods for studies of snake ecology and conservation." *Snakes: ecology and conservation* 1 (2009): 5–37.

Dragusanu, Raluca, Montero, Eduardo, and Nathan Nunn. "The effects of fair trade certification: Evidence from coffee producers in Costa Rica." Working Paper 24260 http://www.nber.org/papers/w24260, August 2021.

Escobar-Ramírez, Selene, Teja Tscharntke, Inge Armbrecht, Wilmar Torres, and Ingo Grass. "Decrease in β-diversity, but not in α-diversity, of ants in intensively managed coffee plantations." *Insect Conservation and Diversity* 13, no. 5 (2020): 445–455.

Estow, Clara. "Reflections on gold: On the late medieval background of the Spanish 'enterprise of the Indies.'" *Mediaevistik* 6 (1993): 85–120.

Fair Trade Uk. "Coffee farmers." 2022. https://www.fairtrade.org.uk/farmers-and-workers/coffee/, accessed June 16, 2022.

Ferreira, Francisco, and Marta Schoch. 2020. "Inequality and social unrest in Latin America: The Tocqueville Paradox revisited." February 24, 2022. https://blogs.worldbank.org/developmenttalk/inequality-and-social-unrest-latin-america-tocqueville-paradox-revisited, accessed December 19, 2022.

Ferreira, T., J. Shuler, R. Guimaraes, and A. Farah. "Introduction to coffee plant and genetics." In *Coffee: Production, Quality, and Chemistry*, edited by Adriana Farah, 3–25. Croydon, UK: Royal Society of Chemistry, 2019.

Food and Agricultural Organization of the United Nations (FAO). "Markets and trade: Coffee." https://www.fao.org/markets-and-trade/commodities/coffee/en/, accessed June 5, 2023.

Flores-Solórzano, Samia B., Esperanza Huerta-Lwanga, Raúl Cuevas-González, and Karina Guillén-Navarro. "Optimal conditions to produce extracts of compost and vermicompost from oil palm and coffee pulp wastes." *Journal of Material Cycles and Waste Management* 24, 2(2022): 801–810. https://doi.org/10.1007/s10163-022-01365-1.

Forero Alvarez, Jaime. "Colombian family farmers' adaptations to new conditions in the world coffee market." *Latin American Perspectives* 171 (2010): 93–110.

Fresneda, Edel J. "Cuba, development, Dependency, and Structural Heterogeneity." *Problemas del Desarrollo* 47, no. 187 (2016): 113–138.

Furlong, William L. "Costa Rica: Caught between two worlds." *Journal of Interamerican Studies and World Affairs* 29, no. 2 (1987): 119–154.

Gallina, S., S. Mandujano, and A. González-Romero. "Conservation of mammalian biodiversity in coffee plantations of Central Veracruz, Mexico." *Agroforestry Systems* 33 (1996): 13–27.

García-Cárdenas, Delly Rocío, Inge Armbrecht, Wilmar Torres, Martha L. Baena, and James Montoya-Lerma. "Functional significance of the leaf-cutting ant *Atta cephalotes* (Formicidae) in coffee plantations: An enemy or an ally?" *Pedobiologia* 93–94 (2022): 150825. https://doi.org/10.1016/j.pedobi.2022.150825.

Garcia, Flávio R. M., Sérgio M. Ovruski, Lorena Suárez, Jorge Cancino, and Oscar E. Liburd. "Biological control of tephritid fruit flies in the Americas and Hawaii: A review of the use of parasitoids and predators." *Insects* 11, no. 10 (2020): 662.

Garibaldi, Lucas A., Ingolf Steffan-Dewenter, Rachael Winfree, Marcelo A. Aizen, Riccardo Bommarco, Saul A. Cunningham, Claire Kremen, Luísa G. Carvalheiro, Lawrence D. Harder, Ohad Afik, Ignasi Bartomeus, Faye Benjamin, Virginie Boreux, Daniel Cariveau, Natacha P. Chacoff, Jan H. Dudenhöffer, Breno M. Freitas, Jaboury Ghazoul, Sarah Greenleaf, Juliana Hipólito, Andrea Holzschuh, Brad Howlett, Rufus Isaacs, Steven K. Javorek, Christina M. Kennedy, Kristin M. Krewenka, Smitha Krishnan, Yael Mandelik, Margaret M. Mayfield, Iris Motzke, Theodore Munyuli, Brian A. Nault, Mark Otieno, Jessica Petersen, Gideon Pisanty, Simon G. Potts, Romina Rader, Taylor H. Ricketts, Maj Rundlöf, Colleen L. Seymour, Christof Schüepp, Hajnalka Szentgyörgyi, Hisatomo Taki, Teja Tscharntke, Carlos H. Vergara, Blandina F. Viana, Thomas C. Wanger, Catrin Westphal, Neal Williams, and Alexandra M. Klein. "Wild pollinators enhance fruit set of crops regardless of honey bee abundance." *Science* 339, 6127 (2013): 1608–1611. https://doi.org/10.1126/science.1230200.

Goldberg, T. L., T. K. Anderson, and G. L. Hamer. "West Nile virus may have hitched a ride across the Western United States on *Culex tarsalis* mosquitoes." *Molecular Ecology* 198 (2010): 1518–1519.

Gonzalez, Victor. 2020. "Coffee Annual." United States Department of Agriculture-Foreign Agricultural Service. https://apps.fas.usda.gov/newgainapi/api/Report/DownloadReportByFileName?fileName=Coffee%20Annual_San%20Jose_Costa%20Rica_CS2023-0004.pdf, accessed June 20, 2023.

Grüter, Roman, Tim Trachsel, Patrick Laube, and Isabel Jaisli. "Expected global suitability of coffee, cashew and avocado due to climate change." *PLOS ONE* 17, no. 1 (2022): e0261976. https://doi.org/10.1371/journal.pone.0261976.

Gudmundson, Lowell. *Costa Rica After Coffee: The Co-Op Era in History and Memory*. Baton Rouge: Louisiana State University Press, 2021.

Hall, Carolyn. *Costa Rica: A Geographical Interpretation in Historical Perspective*. Boulder: Westview Press, 1985.

Hamon, Perla, Corrinne E. Grover, Aaron P. Davis, Jean-Jacques Rakotomalala, Nathalie E. Raharimalala, Victor A. Albert, Hosahalli L. Sreenath, Piet Stoffelen, Sharon E. Mitchell, Emmanuel Couturon, Serge Hamon, Alexandre de Kochko, Dominique Crouzillat, Michel Rigoreau, Ucu Sumirat, Sélastique Akaffou, and Romain Guyot. "Genotyping-by-sequencing provides the first well-resolved phylogeny for coffee (Coffea) and insights into the evolution of caffeine content in its species: GBS coffee phylogeny and the evolution of caffeine content." *Molecular Phylogenetics and Evolution* 109 (2017): 351–361. https://doi.org/10.1016/j.ympev.2017.02.009.

Harvey, Celia A., Alyssa A. Pritts, Marie J. Zwetsloot, Kees Jansen, Mirjam M. Pulleman, Inge Armbrecht, Jacques Avelino, Juan F. Barrera, Christian Bunn, Javier Hoyos García, Carlos Isaza, Juana Munoz-Ucros, Carlos J. Pérez-Alemán, Eric Rahn, Valentina Robiglio, Eduardo Somarriba, and Vivian Valencia. "Transformation of coffee-growing landscapes across Latin America. A review." *Agronomy for Sustainable Development* 41, no. 5 (2021): 62. https://doi.org/10.1007/s13593-021-00712-0.

Hensel, Silke. "Africans in Spanish America: Slavery, freedom and identities in the colonial era." *Indiana* 24 (2007): 15–37.

Hidalgo, Juan. "Growth without poverty reduction: The case of Costa Rica." *Cato Institute Economic Development Bulletin* 18 (2014).

Hiltunen Biesanz, Marta, Biesanz, Richard, and Karen Zubris Biesanz. *The Ticos: Culture and Social Change in Costa Rica*. Boulder: Lynne Rienner Publishers, 1999.

Høivik, Tord, and Solveig Aas. "Demilitarization in Costa Rica: A farewell to arms?" *Journal of Peace Research* 18, no. 4 (1981): 333–351.

Holden, Robert H. "Constructing the limits of State Violence: Towards a new research agenda." *Journal of Latin American Studies* 28, no. 2 (1996): 435–459.

Hooks, Cerruti R. R., Raju R. Pandey, and Marshall W. Johnson. "Impact of avian and arthropod predation on lepidopteran caterpillar densities and plant productivity in an ephemeral agroecosystem." *Ecological Entomology* 28, no. 5 (2003): 522–532. https://doi.org/10.1046/j.1365-2311.2003.00544.x.

Hopfensitz, Astrid, and Josepa Miquel-Florensa. "Mill ownership and farmer's cooperative behavior: The case of Costa Rica coffee farmers." *Journal of Institutional Economics* 13, no. 3 (2017): 623–648.

Huang, Ruiqi, Andrew J. O'Donnell, Jessica J. Barboline, and Todd J. Barkman. "Convergent evolution of caffeine in plants by co-option of exapted ancestral enzymes." *Proceedings of the National Academy of Sciences* 113, no. 38 (2016): 10613–10618. https://doi.org/10.1073/pnas.1602575113.

Ijanu, E. M., A. Kamaruddin, and· F. A. Norashiddin. "Coffee processing wastewater treatment: A critical review on current treatment technologies with a proposed alternative." *Applied Water Science* 10, no. 11 (2020). https://doi.org/10.1007/s13201-019-1091-9.

Imbach, Pablo, Emily Fung, Lee Hannah, Carlos E. Navarro-Racines, David W. Roubik, Taylor H. Ricketts, Celia A. Harvey, Camila I. Donatti, Peter Läderach, Bruno

Locatelli, and Patrick R. Roehrdanz. "Coupling of pollination services and coffee suitability under climate change." *Proceedings of the National Academy of Sciences* 114, no. 39 (2017): 10438–10442. https://doi.org/10.1073/pnas.1617940114.

International Coffee Organization. "Annual review coffee year 2019/2020." Overcoming the Pandemic: A Year Unlike Any Other. https://www.ico.org/documents/cy2020-21/annual-review-2019-2020-e.pdf.

Irwin, Douglas A. "The rise and fall of import substitution." Peterson Institute for International Economics, Working Paper 20-10, July, 2020.

Jamieson, Ross W. "The essence of commodification: Caffeine dependencies in the Early Modern World." *Journal of Social History* 35, no. 2 (2001): 269–294.

Jaramillo, Juliana, Eric Muchugu, Fernando E. Vega, Aaron Davis, Christian Borgemeister, and Adenirin Chabi-Olaye. "Some like it hot: The influence and implications of climate change on coffee berry borer (Hypothenemus hampei) and coffee production in East Africa." *PLOS ONE* 6, no. 9 (2011): e24528. https://doi.org/10.1371/journal.pone.0024528.

Jedlicka, Julie A., Russell Greenberg, and Deborah K. Letourneau. "Avian conservation practices strengthen ecosystem services in California Vineyards." *PLOS ONE* 6, no. 11 (2011): e27347.

Johnson, M. D., J. L. Kellermann, and A. M. Stercho. "Pest reduction services by birds in shade and sun coffee in Jamaica." *Animal Conservation* 13, no. 2 (2010): 140–147.

Joliffe, Lee. "Coffee culture, destinations and tourism." (Tourism and Cultural Change, 24) (April 20, 2010).

Jones, Jeffrey R. *Colonization and the Environment: Land Settlement Projects in Central America.* Tokyo: United Nations University Press, 1990.

Kammerichs-Berke, Deven, Fanter J. Lane, Frank Juma Ong'Ondo, Edson M. Mlamba, William T. Bean, Julie A. Jedlicka, Peter Njoroge, and Matthew D. Johnson. "The effect of shade tree species on bird communities in central Kenyan coffee farms." *Bird Conservation International* 32, no. 4 (2022): 655–673. https://doi.org/10.1017/S0959270921000502.

Karp, Daniel S., and Gretchen C. Daily. "Cascading effects of insectivorous birds and bats in tropical coffee plantations." *Ecology* 95, no. 4 (2014): 1065–1074. https://doi.org/10.1890/13-1012.1.

Karp, Daniel S, Chase D Mendenhall, Randi Figueroa Sandí, Nicolas Chaumont, Paul R Ehrlich, Elizabeth A Hadly, and Gretchen C Daily. "Forest bolsters bird abundance, pest control and coffee yield." *Ecology Letters* 16, no. 11 (2013): 1339–1347.

Kath, Jarrod, Vivekananda M. Byrareddy, Alessandro Craparo, Thong Nguyen-Huy, Shahbaz Mushtaq, Loc Cao, and Laurent Bossolasco. "Not so robust: Robusta coffee production is highly sensitive to temperature." *Global Change Biology* 26, no. 6 (2020): 3677–3688.

Kellermann, J. L., M. D. Johnson, A. M. Stercho, and S. C. Hackett. "Ecological and economic services provided by birds on Jamaican blue mountain coffee farms." *Conservation Biology* 22, no. 5 (2008): 1177–1185. https://doi.org/10.1111/j.1523-1739.2008.00968.x.

Kerr, Suzi, Alexander Pfaff, and G. Arturo Sanchez-Azofeifa. "Development and deforestation: Evidence from Costa Rica." *Journal of Environment Economics and Management* 7, no. 31 (2003): 1–30.

Kitajima, E. W., and C. M. Chagas. "Viral diseases in coffee." In *Coffee: Growing, Processing, Sustainable Production*, edited by J. N. Wintgens, 546–550. Verlag: Wiley-VCH, 2012.

Klein, A. M., I. Steffan-Dewenter, and T. Tscharntke. "Bee pollination and fruit set of Coffea arabica and C. canephora (Rubiaceae)." *American Journal of Botany* 90, no. 1 (2003): 153–157. https://doi.org/10.3732/ajb.90.1.153.

Klingel, Tizian, Jonathan I. Kremer, Vera Gottstein, Tabata Rajcic de Rezende, Steffen Schwarz, and Dirk W. Lachenmeier. "A review of coffee by-products including leaf, flower, cherry, husk, silver skin, and spent grounds as novel foods within the European Union." *Foods* 9, no. 5 (2020): 665.

Knight, Alan. "The great depression in Latin America: An overview." In *The Great Depression in Latin America*, edited by Paulo Drinot and Alan Knight, 276–339. Durhan: Duke University Press, 2014.

Koch, Charles W. "Jamaican blacks and their descendants in Costa Rica." *Social and Economic Studies* 26, no. 3 (September 1977): 339–361.

Lange, Matthew, Mahoney, James, and Mattias vom Hau. "Colonialism and development: A comparative analysis of Spanish and British Colonies." *American Journal of Sociology* 111, no. 5 (2006): 1412–1462.

Lehoucq, Fabrice Edouard. "Class conflict, political crisis and the breakdown of democratic practices in Costa Rica: Reassessing the origins of the 1948 Civil War." *Journal of Latin American Studies* 23 (1991): 37–60.

Leibrock, Nils V., Joris Santegoets, Paul J. W. Mooijman, Filemon Yusuf, Xander C. L. Zuijdgeest, Esmée A. Zutt, Josette G. M. Jacobs, and Jan G. Schaart. "The biological feasibility and social context of gene-edited, caffeine-free coffee." *Food Science and Biotechnology* 31, no. 6 (2022): 635–655. https://doi.org/10.1007/s10068-022-01082-3.

Leroy, T., A. M. Henry, M. Royer, I. Altosaar, R. Frutos, D. Duris, and R. Philippe. "Genetically modified coffee plants expressing the Bacillus thuringiensis cry1Ac gene for resistance to leaf miner." *Plant Cell Reports* 19, no. 4 (2000): 382–385. https://doi.org/10.1007/s002990050744.

Lewis, Nell. "This country regrew its lost forest. Can the world learn from it?" https://www.cnn.com/2020/07/27/americas/reforestation-costa-rica-c2e-spc/index.html, accessed November 22, 2022.

Longley, Kyle. "Resistance and accommodation: The United States and the Nationalism of José Figueres, 1953–1957." *Diplomatic History* 18, no. 1 (Winter 1994): 1–28.

Los Santos Digital. "Café de Tarrazú se dejó los primeros tres lugares de Taza de la Excelencia." Junio 20, 2021. https://lossantosdigital.com/2021/06/18/cafe-de-tarrazu-se-dejo-los-primeros-tres-lugares-de-taza-de-la-excelencia-2021/, accessed February 2, 2023.

Loveman, Brian. *The Constitution of Tyranny: Regimes of Exception in Spanish America.* Pittsburgh: University of Pittsburgh Press, 1993.

Maas, Bea, Daniel S. Karp, Sara Bumrungsri, Kevin Darras, David Gonthier, Joe C. C. Huang, Catherine A. Lindell, Josiah J. Maine, Laia Mestre, Nicole L. Michel, Emily B. Morrison, Ivette Perfecto, Stacy M. Philpott, Çagan H. Şekercioğlu, Roberta M. Silva, Peter J. Taylor, Teja Tscharntke, Sunshine A. Van Bael, Christopher J. Whelan, and Kimberly Williams-Guillén. "Bird and bat predation services in tropical forests and agroforestry landscapes." *Biological Reviews* 91, no. 4 (2016): 1081–1101. https://doi.org/10.1111/brv.12211.

Marín, Linda, and Ivette Perfecto. "Spider diversity in coffee agroecosystems: The influence of agricultural intensification and aggressive ants." *Environmental Entomology* 42, no. 2 (2013): 204–213.

Marino, Yobana A, Victor J Vega, José M García, José C Verle Rodrigues, Noelia M García, and Paul Bayman. "The coffee berry borer (Coleoptera: Curculionidae) in Puerto Rico: Distribution, infestation, and population per fruit." *Journal of Insect Science* 17, no. 2 (2017).

Marquis, R. J., and C. J. Whelan. "Insectivorous birds increase growth of white oak through consumption of leaf-chewing insects." *Ecology* 75 (1994): 2007–2014.

Marquardt, Steve. "Pesticides, parakeets, and unions in the Costa Rican banana industry, 1938–1962." *Latin American Research Review* 37, no. 2 (2002): 3–36.

Martínez-Salinas, Alejandra, Fabrice DeClerck, Kerri Vierling, Lee Vierling, Luc Legal, Sergio Vílchez-Mendoza, and Jacques Avelino. "Bird functional diversity supports pest control services in a Costa Rican coffee farm." *Agriculture, Ecosystems & Environment* 235 (2016): 277–288.

Mata, Francisco J., and Irene Hernández-Ruiz. "CRGOURMETCOFFEE.COM: An E-Commerce platform to solve the coffee paradox in Costa Rica." *IADIS International Journal* 17, no. 2 (2019): 85–103.

Mendenhall, Chase D., Luke O. Frishkoff, Georgina Santos-Barrera, Jesús Pacheco, Eyobed Mesfun, Fernando Mendoza Quijano, Paul R. Ehrlich, Gerardo Ceballos, Gretchen C. Daily, and Robert M. Pringle. "Countryside biogeography of Neotropical reptiles and amphibians." *Ecology* 95, no. 4 (2014): 856–870. https://doi.org/10.1890/12-2017.1.

Mikosch, Elisabeth. "The manufacture and trade of luxury textiles in the age of mercantilism." *Textile Society of America Symposium Proceedings*, 1990.

Moat, Justin, Jenny Williams, Susana Baena, Timothy Wilkinson, Tadesse W. Gole, Zeleke K. Challa, Sebsebe Demissew, and Aaron P. Davis. "Resilience potential of the Ethiopian coffee sector under climate change." *Nature Plants* 3, no. 7 (2017): 17081. https://doi.org/10.1038/nplants.2017.81.

Moguel, P., and V. M. Toledo. "Biodiversity conservation in traditional coffee systems of Mexico." *Conservation Biology* 13 (1999): 11–21.

Monge, Félix. "CoopeTarrazú R.L.: A coffee culture." PowerPoint Presentation, March 21, 2010.

Muñoz Guillen, Mercedes. "Costa Rica: La Abolición del Ejército y la Construcción de la Paz Regional." In *Antología del Pensamiento Crítico Costarricense Contemporáneo*, edited by Sagot, Montserrat and David Díaz Arias, 213–227. 2014.

Munoz, J. C., R. Aerts, K. W. Thijs, P. R. Stevenson, B. Muys, and C. H. Sekercioglu. "Contribution of woody habitat islands to the conservation of birds and their potential ecosystem services in an extensive Colombian rangeland." *Agriculture, Ecosystems & Environment* 173 (2013): 13–19. https://doi.org/10.1016/j.agee.2013.04.006.

Murillo, Alvaro. 2020. "Costa Rican coffee may go unharvested as pandemic creates migrant worker shortage." https://www.reuters.com/article/us-health-coronavirus-costa-rica-coffee/costa-rican-coffee-may-go-unharvested-as-pandemic-creates-migrant-worker-shortage-idUSKBN2411W9, accessed December 19, 2022.

Murthy, Pushpa S., and M. Madhava Naidu. "Sustainable management of coffee industry by-products and value addition—A review." *Resources, Conservation and Recycling* 66 (2012): 45–58.

Muschler, R. G. "Shade management and its effect on coffee growth and quality." In *Coffee: Growing, Processing, Sustainable Production*, edited by J. N. Wintgens, 391–418. Verlag: Wiley-VCH, 2004.

Naivo Cafe. "What is India Monsoon Malabar? A complete brewing and roasting guide." https://naivo.in/blog/what-is-indian-monsoon-malabar-coffee, accessed January 23, 2023.

NASDAQ. Coffee Prices. https://www.nasdaq.com/market-activity/commodities/kt:nmx, accessed June 26, 2023.

Nathanson, James A. "Caffeine and related methylxanthines: Possible naturally occurring pesticides." *Science* 226, no. 4671 (1984): 184–187.

Nohlen, Dieter. *Elections in the Americas: A Data Handbook*, Volume One. Oxford: Oxford University Press, 2005.

Olander, Marcia. "Costa Rica in 1948: Cold war or local war?" *The Americas* 52, no. 4 (April 1996): 465–493.

Osorio, Néstor. "Lessons from the world coffee crisis: A serious for sustainable development." International Coffee Organization. Submission to UNCTAD XI, São Paulo, Brazil, June 2004.

Ovalle-Rivera, Oriana, Peter Läderach, Christian Bunn, Michael Obersteiner, and Götz Schroth. "Projected shifts in Coffea arabica suitability among major global producing regions due to climate change." *PLOS ONE* 10, no. 4 (2015): e0124155.

Paddle.com. "How starbucks uses pricing strategy for profit maximization." https://www.paddle.com/blog/starbucks-pricing-strategy, accessed February 15, 2024.

Paige, Jeffery M. *Coffee and Power: Revolution and the Rise of Democracy in Central America.* Cambridge: Harvard University Press, 1997.

Paige, Jeffery M. "Conjuncture, comparison, and conditional theory in macrosocial inquiry." *American Journal of Sociology* 105, no. 3 (1999): 781–800.

PBS.org. "How many slaves landed in the US?" https://www.pbs.org/wnet/african-americans-many-rivers-to-cross/history/how-many-slaves-landed-in-the-us/, accessed June 21, 2022. "Do consumers care about ethics? Willingness to pay for fair-trade coffee." *The Journal of Consumer Affairs* 39, no. 2 (2005): 363–385.

Pendergrast, Mark. *Uncommon Grounds: The History of Coffee and How it Transformed Our World.* Basic Books, 2010.

Perelló, Lucas, and Patricio Navia. "Abrupt and gradual realignments: The case of Costa Rica 1958–2018." *Journal of Politics in Latin America* 13, no. 1 (2021): 86–113.

Perfecto, Ivette, and John Vandermeer. "The effect of an ant-hemipteran mutualism on the coffee berry borer (Hypothenemus hampei) in southern Mexico." *Agriculture, Ecosystems & Environment* 117, no. 2 (2006): 218–221. https://doi.org/10.1016/j.agee.2006.04.007.

Perfecto, Ivette, Zachary Hajian-Forooshani, Alexa White, and John Vandermeer. "Ecological complexity and contingency: Ants and lizards affect biological control of the coffee leaf miner in Puerto Rico." *Agriculture, Ecosystems & Environment* 305 (2021): 107104. https://doi.org/10.1016/j.agee.2020.107104.

Pham, Yen, Kathryn Reardon-Smith, Shahbaz Mushtaq, and Geoff Cockfield. "The impact of climate change and variability on coffee production: a systematic review." *Climatic Change* 156, no. 4 (2019): 609–630. https://doi.org/10.1007/s10584-019-02538-y.

Prnewswire. 2022. "Coffee consumption hits two-decade high - Spring 2022 National Coffee Data Trends report." https://www.prnewswire.com/news-releases/coffee-consumption-hits-two-decade-high-spring-2022-national-coffee-data-trends-report-301502866.html, accessed June 15, 2022.

Quesada-Román, Adolfo, Quirós-Arias, Lilliam, and Juan Carlos Zamora-Pereira. "Interactions between Geomorphology and production chain of high-quality coffee in Costa Rica." *Sustainability* 14 (2022): 1–15.

Quirós, Claudia. "Hunting Indians." In *The Costa Rica Reader: History, Culture, Politics*, edited by Palmer, Steven and Iván Molina, 16–21. Duke University Press: Durham, 2004.

Rainforest Alliance. https://www.rainforest-alliance.org/, accessed June 9, 2023.

Rao, Maya V, Robert A Rice, Robert C Fleischer, and Carly R Muletz-Wolz. "Soil fungal communities differ between shaded and sun-intensive coffee plantations in El Salvador." *PLOS ONE* 15, no. 4 (2020): e0231875.

Reuters. "Coffee farmers struggle to curb roya outbreak in Central America." 2013. https://www.reuters.com/article/centralamerica-coffee/coffee-farmers-struggle-to-curb-roya-outbreak-in-central-america-idUSL1E9CBCZW20130117, accessed December 18, 2022.

Reuters. "Coffee crisis in central America Fuels Exodus North." 2021. https://www.reuters.com/markets/commodities/coffee-crisis-central-america-fuels-record-exodus-north-2021-12-08/, accessed December 18, 2022.

Roberts, Dina L., Robert J. Cooper, and Lisa J. Petit. "Flock characteristics of ant-following birds in premontane moist forest and coffee agroecosystems." *Ecological Applications* 10, no. 5 (2000): 1414–1425. https://doi.org/10.2307/2641295.

Rodríguez-San Pedro, Annia, Juan Luis Allendes, Clemente A. Beltrán, Pascal N. Chaperon, Mónica M. Saldarriaga-Córdoba, Andrea X. Silva, and Audrey A. Grez. "Quantifying ecological and economic value of pest control services provided by bats in a vineyard landscape of central Chile." *Agriculture, Ecosystems & Environment* 302 (2006): 107063. https://doi.org/10.1016/j.agee.2020.107063.

Roseberry, William. "La Falta de Brazos: Land and labor in the coffee economies of nineteenth-century Latin America." *Theory and Society* 20, no. 3 (1991): 351–381.

Rosenberg, Mark B. "Social reform in Costa Rica: Social security and the presidency of rafael angel Calderón." *The Hispanic American Historical Review* 61, no. 2 (May 1981): 278–296.

Rosenberg, Mark B. "Social security policymaking in Costa Rica: A research report." *Latin American Research Review* 14, no. 1 (1979): 116–133.

Roubik, David W. "The value of bees to the coffee harvest." *Nature* 417, no. 6890 (2002): 708–708.

Samper, Mario. "Costa Rica's response to the coffee crisis." *Latin American Perspectives* 37, no. 2 (2010): 72–92.

Schmitt, Christine B., Feyera Senbeta, Manfred Denich, Helmut Preisinger, and Hans Juergen Boehmer. "Wild coffee management and plant diversity in the montane rainforest of southwestern Ethiopia." *African Journal of Ecology* 48, no. 1 (2010): 78–86. https://doi.org/10.1111/j.1365-2028.2009.01084.x.

Schneider, Elena. "African slavery and Spanish empire" imperial imaginings and bourbon reform in eighteenth-century Cuba and Beyond." *Journal of Early American History* 5 (2015): 3–29.

Schwenk, W. S., A. M. Strong, and T. S. Sillett. 2010. "Effects of bird predation on arthropod abundance and tree growth across an elevational gradient." *Journal of Avian Biology* 41, no. 4 (2010): 367–377. https://doi.org/10.1111/j.1600-048X.2009.04963.x.

Şekercioğlu, C. H. "Promoting community-based bird monitoring in the tropics: Conservation, research, environmental education, capacity-building, and local incomes." *Biological Conservation* 151, no. 1 (2012): 69–73. https://doi.org/10.1016/j.biocon.2011.10.024.

Sekercioglu, Cagan H., Scott R. Loarie, Federico Oviedo Brenes, Paul R. Ehrlich, and Gretchen C. Daily. "Persistence of forest birds in the Costa Rican agricultural countryside." *Conservation Biology* 21, no. 2 (2007): 482–494.

Şekercioğlu, Çağan H., Chase D. Mendenhall, Federico Oviedo-Brenes, Joshua J. Horns, Paul R. Ehrlich, and Gretchen C. Daily. "Long-term declines in bird populations in tropical agricultural countryside." *Proceedings of the National Academy of Sciences* 116, no. 20 (2019): 9903–9912.

Seligson, Mitchell. "Agrarian policies in dependent societies: Costa Rica." *Journal of Interamerican Studies and World Affairs* 19, no. 2 (May 1977): 201–232.

Seligson, Mitchell. *Peasants of Costa Rica & the Development of Agrarian Capitalism.* Madison: The University of Wisconsin Press, 1980.

Seligson, Mitchell. "Democratic stability and economic crisis: Costa Rica, 1978–1983." *International Studies Quarterly* 31 (1987): 301–326.

Seligson, Mitchell A., and Booth, John A. "Political culture and regime type: Evidence from Nicaragua and Costa Rica." *The Journal of Politics* 55, no. 3 (August 1993): 777–792.

Sherman, L. A., and Brye, K. R. "Soil chemical property changes in response to long-term pineapple cultivation in Costa Rica." *Agrosystems, Geosciences & Environment* 2 (2019): 1–9 190052. https://doi.org/10.2134/age2019.07.0052.

Sinu, Palatty Allesh, Gopika Viswan, P. P. Fahira, T. P. Rajesh, K. Manoj, M. Hariraveendra, and Thomas Jose. "Shade tree diversity may not drive prey-predator interaction in coffee agroforests of the Western Ghats biodiversity hotspot, India." *Biological Control* 160 (2021): 104674. https://doi.org/10.1016/j.biocontrol.2021.104674.

Smith, S. D. "Accounting for taste: British coffee consumption in historical perspective." *The Journal of Interdisciplinary History* 27, no. 2 (1996): 183–214.

Snoeck, D., and P. Vaast. "Importance of organic matter and biological fertility in coffee soils." In *Coffee: Growing, Processing, and Sustainable Production*, edited by J. N. Witgens, 371–383. Verlag: Wiley-VCH, 2004.

Snoeck, J., and Ch. Lambot. "Crop maintenance." In *Coffee: Growing, Processing, Sustainable Production*, edited by J. N. Wintgens, 250–273. Weinheim: Wiley-VCH, 2012.

Soto-Pinto, Lorena, Yolanda Romero-Alvarado, Javier Caballero-Nieto, and Gerardo Segura Warnholtz. 2001. "Woody plant diversity and structure of shade-grown-coffee plantations in Northern Chiapas, Mexico." *Revista de Biología Tropical* 49, (2001): 977–987.

Stone, Irving. "British direct and portfolio investment in Latin America before 1914." *The Journal of Economic History* 37, no. 3 (1977): 690–722.

Summers, Chris. "Home Vietnam became a coffee giant." January 14, 2014. https://www.bbc.com/news/magazine-25811724, accessed December 19, 2022.

Thorning, Joseph F. "The Costa Rican story." *World Affairs* 112, no. 2 (1949): 49–50.

Tico Times. "With no official residence to call home, Costa Rica's president keeps his humble digs." 2014. https://ticotimes.net/2014/05/14/with-no-official-residence-to-call-home-costa-ricas-president-keeps-his-humble-digs, accessed June 22, 2023.

Topik, Steven. "The world coffee market in the eighteenth and nineteenth centuries, from Colonial to National Regimes." *Working Paper no. 04/04*, University of California, Irvine, 2004.

Toohey, Ryan C., Jan Boll, Erin S. Brooks, and Jeffrey R. Jones. "Effects of land use on soil properties and hydrological processes at the point, plot, and catchment scale in volcanic soils near Turrialba, Costa Rica." *Geoderma* 315 (2018): 138–148. https://doi.org/10.1016/j.geoderma.2017.11.044.

Topik, Steven, Carlos Marichal, and Zephyr Frank, eds. *From Silver to Cocaine: Latin American Commodity Chains and the Building of the World Economy, 1500–2000*. Durham: Duke University Press, 2006.

Tournebize, Rémi, Leyli Borner, Stéphanie Manel, Christine N. Meynard, Yves Vigouroux, Dominique Crouzillat, Coralie Fournier, Mohamed Kassam, Patrick Descombes, Christine Tranchant-Dubreuil, Hugues Parrinello, Catherine Kiwuka, Ucu Sumirat, Hyacinthe Legnate, Jean-Léon Kambale, Bonaventure Sonké, Jose Cassule Mahinga, Pascal Musoli, Steven B. Janssens, Piet Stoffelen, Alexandre de Kochko, and Valérie Poncet. "Ecological and genomic vulnerability to climate change across native populations of Robusta coffee (Coffea canephora)." *Global Change Biology* 28, no. 13 (2022): 4124–4142. https://doi.org/10.1111/gcb.16191.

Tucker, Catherine M. *Coffee Culture: Local Experiences, Global Connections*, 2nd Edition. New York: Routledge, 2017.

Traore, Togo M, N. L. W. Wilson, and Deague Fields III. "What explains speciality coffee scores and prices: A case study from the cup of excellence program." *Journal of Agricultural and Applied Economics* 50, no. 3 (2018): 349–368.

Twomey, Michael J. "The 1930s depression in Latin America: A macro analysis." *Explorations in Economic History* 20 (1983): 221–247.

Twomey, Michael J. "The debt crisis and Latin America agriculture." *The Journal of Developing Areas* 23 (1989): 545–566.

United States Department of Agriculture, Foreign Agriculture Service. (USDA) Coffee Annual-Costa Rica, Report #CS2022-0008, May 12, 2022.

United States Department of State. "2022 investment climate statements: Costa Rica. https://www.state.gov/reports/2022-investent-climate-statements/costa-rica/, accessed June 16, 2023.

Van Bael, S. A., P. Bichier, and R. Greenberg. "Bird predation on insects reduces damage to the foliage of cocoa trees (*Theobroma cacao*) in western Panama." *Journal of Tropical Ecology* 23 (2007): 715–719.

Van Bael, Sunshine A., Jeffrey D. Brawn, and Scott K. Robinson. "Birds defend trees from herbivores in a Neotropical forest canopy." *Proceedings of the National Academy of Sciences* 100, no. 14 (2003): 8304–8307.

Vanden Abeele, Samuel, Steven B. Janssens, Justin Asimonyio Anio, Yves Bawin, Jonas Depecker, Bienfait Kambale, Ithé Mwanga Mwanga, Tshimi Ebele, Salvator Ntore, Piet Stoffelen, and Filip Vandelook. "Genetic diversity of wild and cultivated Coffea canephora in northeastern DR Congo and the implications for conservation." *American Journal of Botany* 108, no. 12 (2021): 2425–2434. https://doi.org/10.1002/ajb2.1769.

Venette, Robert C., and William D. Hutchison. "Invasive insect species: Global challenges, strategies & opportunities." *Frontiers in Insect Science* 1 (2021). https://doi.org/10.3389/finsc.2021.650520.

Vogt, Melissa. *Variance in Approach Toward a 'Sustainable' Coffee Industry in Costa Rica: Perspectives from Within; Lessons and Insights.* London: Ubiquity Press, 2019.

Voorend, Koen. ¿Un imán de bienestar en el Sur? Migración y política social en Costa Rica. San José, Costa Rica: Universidad de Costa Rica, 2019.

Waller, J. M., M. Bigger, and R. J. Hillocks. "World coffee production." In *Coffee Pests, Diseases and their Management*, 17–33. CABI Wallingford UK, 2007.

Walters, Christina, and Valerie C Pence. "The unique role of seed banking and cryobiotechnologies in plant conservation." *Plants, People, Planet* 3, no. 1 (2021): 83–91.

Wild, Antony. *Coffee: A Dark History.* New York: W.W. Norton, 2004.

Willer, Helga, Julia Lernoud, and Laura Kemper. "The world of organic agriculture 2018: Summary." In *The World of Organic Agriculture. Statistics and Emerging Trends 2018*, edited by Helga Waller and Julia Lernoud, 22–31. Research Institute of Organic Agriculture FiBL and IFOAM-Organics International.

Winson, Anthony. "Confronting the coffee oligarchy: The roots of Costa Rica's middle road." *Canadian Journal of Latin American and Caribbean Studies* 9, no. 17 (1984): 33–50.

Wintgens, J. N., and F. Descroix. "Establishing a coffee plantation." In *Coffee: Growing, Processing, Sustainable Production*, edited by J. N. Wintgens, 182–248. Weinheim, Germany: Wiley-VCH, 2012.

World Bank. The World by Income and Region. https://datatopics.worldbank.org/world-development-indicators/the-world-by-income-and-region.html, accessed June 24, 2022.

World Bank. Gini Coefficient. https://data.worldbank.org/indicator/SI.POV.GINI?most_recent_value_desc=true, accessed June 24, 2022.

World Bank. "Risk and finance in the coffee sector: A compendium of case studies related to improving risk management and access to finance in the coffee sector." Agricultural Global Practice Paper 02, Report 93923-GLB. (February 2015).

World Economic Forum. "From plant to paper cup: The economics of coffee in one chart. https://www.weforum.org/agenda/2020/10/economics-coffee-cup-costs-break-down, accessed February 9, 2023.

World Integrated Trade Solution. 2022. https://wits.worldbank.org/countrysnapshot/en/CRI, accessed December 8, 2022.

World Justice Project. "The rule of law in Costa Rica: Key findings from the general population poll 2022." https://worldjusticeproject.org/sites/default/files/rule-of-law/costa-rica-2022/Costa_Rica_Report_WJP.pdf?v=1.1, accessed June 19, 2023.

Wright, G. A., D. D. Baker, M. J. Palmer, D. Stabler, J. A. Mustard, E. F. Power, A. M. Borland, and P. C. Stevenson. "Caffeine in floral nectar enhances a pollinator's memory of reward." *Science* 339, no. 6124 (2013): 1202–1204.

Yeager, Timothy J. "Encomienda or slavery: The Spanish crown's choice of labor organization in sixteenth-century Spanish America." *The Journal of Economic History* 55, no. 4 (1995): 842–859.

Zamarripa, A., and V. Pétiard. "Biotechnologies applied to coffee." In *Coffee: Growing, Processing, Sustainable Production* edited by J. N. Witgens, 137–163. Verlag: Wiley-VCH, 2004.

Zhao, Qingyun, Wu Xiong, Yizhang Xing, Yan Sun, Xingjun Lin, and Yunping Dong. "Long-term coffee monoculture alters soil chemical properties and microbial communities." *Scientific Reports* 8, no. 1 (2018): 1–11.

Index

About the Authors

Andrew P. Miller is a professor of political science at Wilkes University in Wilkes-Barre, Pennsylvania. He teaches and researches issues of economic and political development in Central America, with a focus on issues related to the coffee industry and ecotourism. He is also passionate about study abroad and has led over twenty student trips to places like Costa Rica, Nicaragua, Panama, and the Dominican Republic. A native of Illinois, Andy holds a BA from Illinois College, an MA from Illinois State University, and a PhD from Purdue University.

Jeffrey A. Stratford is a professor of biology and current chair of the Biology and Earth System Sciences Department at Wilkes University, where he has been teaching ecology, biostatistics, conservation biology, and ornithology for over fifteen years. Originally from rural New Jersey (yes, there is such a place), Jeff went on to study biology at Rutgers University, earned a master's working on tropical birds at Southeastern Louisiana University, and then a doctorate in ecology from Auburn University. His current research focuses on food webs and forest management.

www.ingramcontent.com/pod-product-compliance
Ingram Content Group UK Ltd.
Pitfield, Milton Keynes, MK11 3LW, UK
UKHW020208290926
15470UKWH00001B/63

9 781666 912791